# An insight into shame

# An insight into
# **shame**

Heather Churchill and Claire Musters

WAVERLEY ABBEY INSIGHT SERIES

## WAVERLEY ABBEY INSIGHT SERIES

The *Waverley Abbey Insight Series* has been developed in response to the great need to help people understand and face some key issues that many of us struggle with today. CWR's ministry spans teaching, training and publishing, and this series draws on all of these areas of ministry.

Sourced from material first presented over Insight Days by CWR, presenters and authors have worked in close co-operation to bring this series together, offering clear insight, teaching and help on a broad range of subjects and issues. Bringing biblical understanding and insight, these books are written both for those who help others and those who face these issues themselves.

Where case studies are included, names and details have been changed to protect the identity of the people concerned. Permission has been given for the stories to be told.

DEDICATION

We often want shame to be healed on its own, but the truth is that we receive the most healing from shame as we receive love, compassion and kindness from others – whether from friends and relations, fellow Christians or from the Lord Himself. I would like to dedicate this book to my husband, who, for 44 years, has shown me lots of love, patience, compassion and unconditional acceptance and who has provided me with much healing from my past shame.

**Heather**

I would also like to dedicate this book to my husband, who, during the most shameful episode of my past, extended love, grace and compassion to me in such a way that I began to understand, appreciate and accept Jesus' love much more deeply. I have come to truly recognise that God loves us unconditionally, and He has helped me to walk away from the shame that could have continued to grip hold of my life.

**Claire**

# Contents

# Foreword

I recall coming to a crossroads in the life and ministry of CWR some years ago, asking God whether we should carry on doing more of the same, or if He was calling us to strike out to fulfil the next steps in His purposes. He revealed to us a considerably more challenging vision of establishing a professionally recognised and academically accredited training course in the field of counselling; one that would be centred on a Christian world-view and underpinned by God's Word with application to everyday life. This is when I met with Heather Churchill and asked her to help us reach out for more.

I'm unsure as to whether either of us were completely aware of the journey ahead: the potholes, twists, turns and the numerous blind corners that were going to be found along the road. Yet today, some years on, with Heather's clinical and academic expertise, tenacity and attention to the smallest detail, we have negotiated the rigours of the many regularity bodies and have established Waverley Abbey College, where currently around 180 students are enrolled in undergraduate and postgraduate counselling programmes registered with Middlesex University. I recognise there is still a significant distance to travel as we seek to add research elements and offer training for further allied people-helping professions, continually seeking to deepen our understanding of who we are in God and how we can see this at work in everyday life and relationships.

In this book, Heather combines her extraordinary attention to detail with her compassion and significant clinical experience, to provide insights into this potentially pernicious and crippling issue of shame. Over the years, we have discussed our shared view that shame is one of the core, underlying struggles of humanity. Its effects are insidious and pervasive. It wears many faces, triggering a whole range of reactions and responses. Because of shame's many presentations, we are often lured into focusing on the more obvious and immediate struggles, while shame manages to bury deeper into the personality, waiting for an opportunity to disrupt our relationships and equilibrium. Shame can create a destructive cycle within the personality, affecting us psychologically, relationally and physiologically.

I wonder if shame could be aptly described as the ultimate disconnection from God and each other. It is surely one of the states of the human condition that is most contrary to our original design, causing us to hide – and, in our hiding, we attempt to numb the pain. In so doing, we cast ourselves a narrow band of emotions, causing us to view the world through grey-tinted glasses, with drab monotone hues and very little depth of field, instead of the ultra-high definition of the three-dimensional, vibrant, full-colour life we read of in the Scriptures.

Heather and Claire helpfully unpack these considerations, and help us to understand the subtle yet important differences between guilt and shame, while offering both helpful and practical ways of releasing ourselves from the grip of shame and stepping into hope and healing.

**Mick Brooks**
CWR Chief Executive

# Introduction

Shame is something that cannot be seen and yet can have huge (often devastating) consequences in our lives. As we will be exploring in the book, our childhood experiences often inform how we respond to the threat of shame in our adult lives. Both Heather and Claire share how they can see that at work in their own lives, and there are many other examples given within case studies throughout the book.

*Insight into Shame* actually began as a seminar that Heather ran for CWR at Waverley Abbey House, which Claire attended. While there, Claire experienced first-hand how many of the delegates had moments of understanding as to why they responded to certain situations in particular ways. She also began to understand some of her own behaviour, and gained real insight into particular interactions she has had with people she is pastorally responsible for.

Heather was able to explain the various different responses we can have when we feel the threat of shame, and provided helpful ways to calm ourselves. As a counsellor, she has found the work of some psychologists particularly helpful, so she explained their ideas in a clear, straightforward way.

In this book, we begin by looking at what shame is, and why it is so often confused with guilt. We also provide a theological understanding of shame; as Christians we believe it is vital to bring this in early on. We then look at how shame develops, through the discipline of psychology, before going on to share some strategies that Heather has found work well with clients, including learning to self-soothe and understanding the child and adult parts of ourselves. The final two chapters focus on how we can bring our faith more fully into the process of recognising and letting go of past shame.

The Waverley Integrative Framework is a really helpful way of explaining how we are each made up of various areas, including physical, cognitive, emotional, behavioural and spiritual, and that each one affects the others. Using this as a basis, we also look at how Jesus is the perfect model of a healthy person and what we can learn from Him. Ultimately, it is as we learn more about, and begin to accept God's complete love and acceptance of us, that we can combat lies and walk free from shame to be the people that God has created us to be. That is our prayer for the book: that those reading it will find some real nuggets of truth that help them in their own life journey.

This book is aimed at individuals who know they struggle with shame, as well as counsellors, pastoral workers and others who are helping people work through shame. As we say in the book, God is our ultimate healer and He chooses to work with each one of us individually in very different ways. We have included techniques and suggestions that we have found helpful for ourselves and clients, but you may well find that particular ones suit you better than others. Please feel free to concentrate on those. Whatever you do, we invite you to include God in the process and be open to what He might want to do to aid healing. His Holy Spirit can help bring understanding and clarity as you look back at your childhood and seek to understand why you respond in the way that you do today.

**Heather and Claire, 2019**

## CHAPTER 1

# What is shame?

Even with the steep rise in mental health issues recently, not all of us will experience what it feels like to suffer from depression or anxiety. It is much more likely, however, that each one of us will suffer from shame at some point in our lives. It is rife – not only in society, but sadly in churches too. But what do we mean by the term 'shame'?

## The far-reaching consequences of shame

Shame is an emotion that has important, far-reaching consequences. Indeed, at times it can have a knock-on effect and make our lives feel unbearable, because we can end up in a destructive cycle of feeling shameful about experiencing shame. It can impact a person psychologically; shame has been linked with a number of emotional and mental health difficulties such as depression, anxiety, stress, eating disorders, addictions.[1]

Shame can also have an impact physiologically, which means it directly affects our physicality. Research in the last few years has suggested that shame can trigger increases in the levels of the stress hormone cortisol, which in turn can lead to significant physical health problems.[2] For example, increases in cortisol have been shown to result in increased heart rate, headaches, high blood pressure and even more serious health conditions such as heart disease.[3]

## A theological understanding of shame

As Christians, there is also a theological aspect to shame that it is helpful to grasp. The first instance of human beings experiencing shame in Scripture can be traced back to Adam and Eve in the Garden of Eden. They began their existence shame-free: 'Adam and his wife were both naked, and they felt no shame' (Gen. 2:25). But, as they ate the fruit that God said was forbidden, 'At that moment their eyes were opened, and they suddenly felt shame at their nakedness. So they sewed fig leaves together to cover themselves' (Gen. 3:7, NLT). When God next visited them in the garden, He had to call out for Adam, who was hiding. Adam responded by explaining: 'I heard you in the garden, and I was afraid because I was naked; so I hid' (v10).

Before they ate the fruit, Adam and Eve were happy as they were, but having eaten it they were aware of their nakedness and experienced a new emotion for the first time: being ashamed.[4] Their response was to cover themselves and try to hide away from God. It is interesting to note that the roots of the word shame are thought to derive from an older word meaning 'to cover'.[5]

Because of their disobedience, Adam and Eve experienced feelings of shame and guilt. Whether we take a literal reading of the text or see it as an explanation of sin entering the world, we can say that sin impacted the world catastrophically and, from that moment onwards, a new emotion, shame, was felt by humanity. We could say, therefore, that shame is a core consequence of the Fall. And its effects are still felt today. It is a universal emotion experienced by *all* human beings – different cultures might have different ways of expressing shame, but the *feeling* is the same.[6]

It is probably fair to say that, historically, Christian theologians have tended to focus on the guilt of Adam and

Eve's actions,[7] thereby minimising the shame impact we've just seen in the Genesis text. This leads us to a crucial question: what is the difference between shame and guilt? Just think for a moment how you would define each; we will look at this in more detail below.

## The difference between shame and guilt

If you sat and thought carefully about it, you may well have come up with a clear difference between the two. The challenge, however, is that often shame and guilt are confused – in society but particularly within church. When this happens, sadly it can cause an unhelpful response to people that are suffering from shame. But why does it happen? Let us consider three possible reasons for this:

- **Feelings**

  It's common for people to confuse the feelings of shame and guilt, as they are so similar. Indeed, numerous writers have pointed out that, in our Western culture, the terms 'shame' and 'guilt' are interchangeable.[8] People can say they feel guilty, even when they have done nothing wrong. For example, survivors of childhood sexual abuse can feel deep guilt for the abuse they suffered as children, which was completely not their fault.[9]

- **Language**

  Our use of language when talking about guilt and shame isn't always helpful either. In the Oxford Dictionary, guilt is defined as 'a feeling of having committed wrong or failed in an obligation'.[10] Shame is 'a painful feeling... caused by the consciousness of wrong or foolish behaviour'.[11] We can see from these definitions how guilt and shame are often put together and that both are frequently viewed in terms of wrong behaviour. For example, we can say to a child who has done something wrong that they should feel guilty, but equally we might say they should be ashamed of themselves, which is confusing and unhelpful.

- **Biblical definitions**
  Attempting a biblical definition of shame can be complex, especially as theologians have historically tended to define shame in terms of sin, guilt and wrong actions, and the need to find forgiveness.[12] Nevertheless, we believe it is absolutely crucial to differentiate between shame and guilt because they are in fact not the same at all. Understanding our own shame, or helping someone else who is struggling with shame, is aided by truly understanding the difference.

We do acknowledge that shame and guilt can co-exist, but it is vital that we grasp this difference: if we are trying to understand our own issues with shame, or trying to help another person, confusing shame with guilt can cause great problems. For instance, Christian pastoral care workers and counsellors have been known to encourage a person who has a problem with shame towards confessing sins and trying to find forgiveness, but that is dealing with their guilt, not with their shame, and could cause more damage. As Christian writers Thomas and Parker state: 'shame and guilt are often confused', and 'a failure to distinguish these emotions leads to ineffective care for those experiencing these emotions'.[13]

Here we explain the difference between them.

## Guilt

Guilt is the instinctive feeling that we are doing, or have done, something against our own value system. We know we are doing something wrong; it's a specific break of the rules and standards we set for ourselves. It can also cause a fear of being found out or fear of punishment – and this can feel very similar to shame. It can also involve feelings of remorse: an unhappiness about what we have done.[14]

Guilt can be seen as helpful and valuable[15] because, for Christians, there is a clear answer to guilt. Guilt has a healthy purpose because it leads us to the cross and helps us to understand our need for forgiveness. If we have done something wrong, experiencing those uncomfortable feelings of guilt leads us to confess that guilt and receive forgiveness, which should bring some form of release. Guilt therefore can be helpful, as accepting you have done wrong and admitting it can be both healthy and healing.[16]

Claire can recognise the value that feeling guilty has had in her marriage, for example. If she has done or said something that she knows has upset her husband, she usually experiences a 'niggle' in her conscience that won't let her rest until she has spoken to him and apologised. The relationship is usually quickly restored and she feels at peace again. The same is true of our relationship with God. The Holy Spirit can even prick our conscience about something that we may not really be aware of, but is blocking our intimacy with God.

Heather can also recall a time when she was at a Christian conference and was talking to another delegate about someone else. When she went back to her room and started to pray, she felt the Holy Spirit convict her that she shouldn't have spoken about that person in the way that she did. She recognised that what she had done was wrong, so asked the Lord for forgiveness. Afterwards, she felt a deep peace and a closeness to God.

## Shame

Shame, on the other hand, is certainly not healthy, and might well be a direct result of us living in a fallen world. For the person who feels a deep sense of shame, it is painful and debilitating – we could in fact say shame can be toxic.[17]

The vital difference is this: shame is about self-evaluation; rather than being about a wrong action, it's more about condemnation of self. It's a deeper experience; a self-conscious emotion.[18] It is not the same as self-esteem, because self-esteem is a rational evaluation of self. So, for example, while guilt focuses on the action we've done as being a mistake, shame tells us that it is our very *being* that is the mistake – who we are.

Shame is what we feel at a heart level about ourselves, and it develops through painful early life experiences. We will explain this in more depth in the next chapter, but for now it's worth recognising that in response to difficult early life events a part of the self says, 'it must be me'. The ongoing message we give ourselves is: 'I am wrong, I am rubbish, I hate myself.' It's not the feeling that we have *done* something wrong, but more the feeling that *we* are wrong.[19] Shame triggers self-condemnation, self-criticism and the desire to hide[20] (as we saw with Adam and Eve).

This in part explains why individuals can experience shame when it is clearly not linked to their own actions.

Mary* had been sexually abused by her father from the age of eight. Over a number of months, Heather worked with Mary and explored with her the deep shame that Mary felt over the abuse she had suffered. Some healing came to Mary as she began to realise, at a heart level, that the abuse was completely not her fault. As Mary rightly started to recognise that the responsibility lay with her father, she began to find some healing. A further breakthrough occurred during therapy when Heather asked Mary what she thought Jesus felt about the abuse. Mary responded by saying she felt that Jesus would be 'on the side of her father'. As Heather explored Mary's instinctive response, Mary slowly became aware that Jesus had a heart and love for little children and that He would have been heartbroken and angry over the abuse that Mary had suffered. After some months, Mary told Heather that she felt her shame had been like 'a dark and heavy cloud that had covered her all her life', but that she now felt it had 'lifted completely off her'.

*All names and details in case studies have been changed.

## Where to start

Psychologists recognise that shame is intrinsically linked with the notion of early broken relationships. This tallies with the scriptural account in the Genesis narrative, where we also see a story of broken relationships. In hiding from God, Adam and Eve were experiencing and demonstrating a separation from Him. They were responding not just to their wrong actions, but also to the shame and broken relationship that had occurred.

So in the Genesis narrative, guilt and shame are interwoven within the context of early broken relationships – between husband and wife (apportioning blame) and God.

To look at another scriptural account, this time in the New Testament, Jesus had an encounter with Zacchaeus in Luke 19:1–10. It is interesting to note that Jesus seemed to deal with Zacchaeus' shame before He dealt with his guilt. Zacchaeus was a tax collector, hated and despised by all, yet Jesus treated him with honour, saying that He wanted to be a guest in his house (which at the time of Jesus was seen as a way of bestowing honour on someone). He was effectively dealing with Zacchaeus' shame about who he was as a person by simply indicating that He was happy to spend time with him. And Zacchaeus' response was to immediately confess and say he wanted to give half his wealth to the poor. He was therefore responding by acknowledging his guilt.

Jesus loved and accepted people where they were. Interestingly, once He had dealt with their sense of shame, individuals often confessed their guilt.

We can learn from Jesus that, whether we are working through our own shame and guilt, or walking alongside someone else doing so, if we focus on dealing with shame first, it can often lead on to looking at healthy guilt and the healing that can come from that too.

## Reflection

While it can be disheartening to read about the way that shame first came into the world, it is important that we recognise its source. The good news is that Jesus came to take away all our guilt and shame. His sacrifice on the cross provides us with forgiveness for our guilt, and also shows us how much we are valued and loved for who we are. Take some time to reflect on that fact before moving on to the next chapter. Here are some scriptures you can use for meditation if you would like to: 1 John 1:9; 3:1; 4:10; Romans 8:1,31–39.

## Activity

Think back over your life – are there clear instances of guilt and shame that you can think of? Is it easier to tell the difference now you are looking back? What about experiences in your early life? Is there anything that you can see as a trigger for you blaming yourself and feeling shame in adulthood?

## Prayer

*Lord, I thank You that I am loved and cherished by You. Help me to truly understand the difference between feelings of guilt, when I need to repent to receive Your forgiveness, and shame, which tries to attack my sense of self. I pray that You will help me to be open to what You want to teach me as I work through this book – for myself but also for others that You want me to help. Amen.*

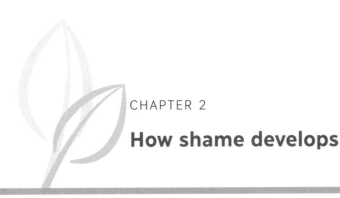

CHAPTER 2

# How shame develops

Psychologists have done a lot of research into shame, and it can be helpful to look at their work as we seek to understand the concept of shame and how it develops.

There are a wide variety of theories that have been developed about shame, such as Jungian, Cognitive Behavioral, Psychodynamic. But, to simplify all their findings, it is probably accurate to say (as indicated earlier) that the emotion of shame is believed by psychologists to be something that is formed early on in childhood. There is now almost universal agreement that the emotion of shame emerges during the toddler stage.[1]

Psychologists believe that shame plays a key role in the development of the self, impacting the way a person views and evaluates themselves. They recognise that children can evaluate from a surprisingly young age and form a 'picture' of themselves, which is basically an internalised view of who they are.[2] Children also develop a view about how others perceive them. In many ways, psychologists would say that the *only* way a child can begin to know themselves is through the eyes of those who are closest to them – generally their parents or main early care givers.[3]

Any difficulties in relationships with care givers will have a huge impact at this stage, as high levels of shame are likely to develop. So we can see that shame is central to a person's developing sense of self.

Relationships with early care givers are not the only

influences on the development of shame. Our early relationships with others can also be influential too, as our own memories of childhood interactions below illustrate.

Claire can still remember two instances at school in which she felt deep shame – just bringing them to mind causes the feelings to resurface. She moved around a lot as a child; having spent some time in America she stood in front of her new class back in England, a few days after a boy from Australia had also started. She was greeted with a boy saying 'not another one' and felt such shame she wanted the ground to swallow her up. She continued to feel like an outsider much of the time. At the same school, she also regularly experienced the dreaded 'walk of shame' over to the PE team that had been forced to take her, as she was the only person not to have been picked to be on a team.

Heather also has an early memory of when she was about four years old. Her class teacher was away so the headmaster was in charge of the class. She was asked to write something and Heather remembers trying really hard to write in her best handwriting. The headmaster walked around the class and stopped when he reached Heather's work. He picked it up, tore it up and put it in the rubbish bin. Heather felt humiliated, embarrassed and ashamed, and picked up a belief that she was not good enough – even at the early age of four.

We are going to move on to look more closely at some of the key theories put forward by psychologists that have contributed to our understanding of the development of shame. Gaining an understanding of how shame develops is key to finding healing for our own struggles with shame and/or if we are trying to help others find healing.

## Freud's response to shame

In his work, Freud considered both guilt and shame, but he was far more concerned with guilt and embarrassment than shame.[4] His focus was on repression: the guilt/embarrassment/shame arising from repression of the sexual drive.[5]

Freud has many critics, not least because his focus tended to be on the frustration of the sex drive. Nevertheless he identified that very young children are basically without shame, and it is difficult early relationships with others that create shame.[6]

## Erik Erikson's Theory of Social Development

The psychologist Erik Erikson was influenced by Freud, but he perceived personality development as a continual process. He outlined eight distinct stages that take place throughout a person's life. Erikson proposed that if any stage is not successfully negotiated, it can cause difficulties. We are particularly interested in Erikson's second stage, Autonomy versus Shame, which occurs around two or three years of age.[7] During this stage, children are struggling to gain a sense of control and independence. If they are affirmed and encouraged, they gain a sense of confidence and security in who they are. However, children who are not given this affirmation are often left with a deep sense of shame and inadequacy.[8] This period is often described as the 'terrible twos', and during this time, children can also experience intense anger and have temper tantrums. Again, if care givers do not assist them, reassure them and encourage them during this stage, they will often have difficulties in regulating (that is, controlling) their emotions. (We will revisit this difficulty again in the next chapter.)

It is also during this stage of development that a child becomes aware of how others perceive them,[9] so the quality of relationship the child holds with their early care givers is extremely important. If they encourage the child to start to become independent, while at the same time protecting them from or helping them deal with failure, all the while conveying empathy, understanding and acceptance as the child starts to explore, then they will develop a healthy sense of who they are. The child will gain a sense of autonomy (a sense of being able to handle problems on their own), as well as a sense of understanding that they are acceptable to themselves and to others. Conversely, if the early care givers ridicule them, are highly critical or don't show love then the child will develop a sense of shame and self-doubt. While it won't necessarily be verbalised, it raises the question in them: is it OK to be me?

> Janet was diagnosed with encopresis around the age of five (which means that she continued to soil herself past the usual age of toilet training). During therapy as an adult, Janet remembered having an accident and soiling herself at a family Christmas party. Her mother smacked her in front of all her aunts and uncles, and Janet felt deeply humiliated and shamed. Janet believed she formed a profound belief about herself from that time on that she was a 'dirty' person, unworthy of love and care from anyone. Though the encopresis was treated and cured around the age of seven, Janet took this core belief into

her adult life, with it impacting most, if not all, of her relationships with others. When she became a Christian in adult life, it also impacted her relationship with God, as she believed that God also saw her as 'dirty' and 'unlovable'. Heather spent much time with Janet in therapy and, gradually, Janet began to understand where her shame came from and why she had formed difficult beliefs about herself. Through time, and much prayer, Janet found healing from her shame and has now gone on to help others with their struggles and difficulties with shame.

## Bowlby's Internal Working Model

John Bowlby (1907–1990) is well known for his formulation and development of Attachment Theory. He perceived that a child's attachment to their early care givers was not only vital for their survival, but also deeply influential in the development of their internal working model (a model of the way a child views themselves, others and their environment). As is shown in the diagram of this working model, if a care giver is uncaring or rejecting or unreliable, the child will develop a working model of self that is unworthy and unlovable. Conversely, if a care giver is loving and kind then a secure attachment is formed and the child develops a working model of self that is worthy and valued.[10]

For those who have painful, abusive childhoods, the internal working model and the relationship with self becomes deeply painful and shameful.[11]

While Bowlby didn't explicitly explore shame in depth, he linked the sense of parents giving the message to a child that they were essentially 'unwanted' to the resulting belief and emotion. This means that as a child develops they get the sense that they are essentially unlovable[12] and therefore develop a deep sense of shame.

A person who constantly feels they are worthless and inadequate can be described as a 'shame prone person'.[13] They will often be in a state of emotional distress with an internal desire to hide.

## Bowlby's Internal Working Model

**If the primary care giver is:**
• Harsh  • Distant  • Unreliable  • Abusive  • Unpredictable

**Then the person's internal view of the world includes:**

| A sense of self as: | A sense of carer as: | A sense of the world as: |
| --- | --- | --- |
| Unworthy | Threatening | |
| Guilty | Anxiety provoking | Dangerous |
| Responsible | Unsafe | Painful |
| Unwanted | Dangerous | Hazardous |
| Unlovable | | |

**But if the care giver is:**
• Consistent  • Reliable  • Available  • Loving  • Responsive

**Then the person's internal view of the world includes:**

| A sense of self as: | A sense of carer as: | A sense of the world as: |
| --- | --- | --- |
| Worthy | Dependable | |
| Valued | Safe | Safe |
| Cared for | Connected | Hopeful |
| Lovable | Nurturing | |

## Reflection

What we have looked at in this chapter reveals that shame is both internal and external. It is external in that it is how we believe others perceive us: what we believe is the image that others have of us in their minds.[14] Coping strategies are developed as a person tries to deal with the difficult responses of early significant care givers.[15] While these strategies are likely to have helped the child survive difficulties in their childhood, they are often outside conscious awareness and become unhelpful in adult life. (We will look more closely at this in the next chapter.) Shame is also internal, because it directly affects the negative way we view ourselves as well as the internal judgments we make about ourselves.[16]

## Activity

Whether you are trying to help someone else overcome shame, or are working through your own, it is really helpful to gain a deeper understanding of how shame develops by taking time to look back over your own childhood. Think about the influence your parents had on your life, and the resulting internal messages you spoke over yourself about your worth. What about your peers too? Were there any significant life events that you know affected how you still feel about yourself today?

## Prayer

*Lord, I am beginning to understand that often the shame that we can carry around with us began to be developed back in childhood. Please help me to be understanding with those I come across who seem to be struggling with shame, and help me to be open to You showing me if there are elements from my own childhood that caused shame to develop in me. Amen.*

CHAPTER 3

# Shame as a threat-based emotion

In order to understand shame further, we will be drawing on various research that has been done in this area. We have already seen that shame is often developed in childhood as a response to different circumstances and experiences. The child develops the unconscious thought that 'it must be me', blaming themselves for what has happened. This belief continues into adult life with the person still blaming themselves, often at an unconscious level.[1]

## The head/heart split

Research suggests that a person suffering from shame usually attacks themselves with rage, self-criticism and self-disgust.[2] This has led some psychologists to suggest that shame is a psychological and physiological response to threat, and that a new approach to dealing with shame is needed.[3]

Let's explain this in more detail. Traditionally, it was thought that shame could be helped by the person telling their story (in order for the memories to be processed). From there, a standard cognitive behavioural therapy (CBT) approach was often used. Using CBT, a therapist would endeavour to help the person observe and identify the negative perceptions and thoughts that they held about themselves and about life events. There would then be an attempt to facilitate a change in thoughts and behaviour in order to reduce emotional distress.[4]

While this approach is not necessarily an unhelpful way of dealing with the feeling of shame and the person's shameful memories, some theorists now believe that rather than help a person change their thoughts and perceptions, it is helpful to understand shame as more of a self-conscious emotion rather than a set of beliefs, and in addition to understand shame as a response to threat.[5] One of the main reasons for dealing with shame in this new and different way is that therapists have often found that when they have tried to help facilitate a person to change their shame beliefs about themselves, they encounter a head/heart spilt. This describes when a person says in their head: 'I know what you are saying is true', but their heart is saying: 'I just don't feel and believe it to be true'.[6] So, a vicious cycle develops where a person continues to feel the same way about themselves and then beats themselves up for feeling that way.[7]

Claire can recognise the head/heart split in herself with old habits she is trying to break. When she slips up she can be very hard on herself – and even when those around her remind her to be more gentle with herself, her response might be to nod her head in agreement, but her heart is still beating her up. She has seen this with people she has been standing with as they seek to deal with shame from the past too. Seeking to step out into their freedom, having processed memories through conversation and prayer, they often then have a battle between what they know in their head and feel in their heart.

Heather has found three different theorists' work particularly helpful as she has sought to work with clients to process their shame and get past this head/heart split. The first is compassion focused therapy, which was developed by Paul Gilbert specifically to address difficulties with shame. The second is the work of Janina Fisher, particularly on healing the fragmented selves of trauma survivors. Finally, Frank Lake's dynamic cycle offers some insights into the spiritual and shame. We will be looking at each of them in turn, with the rest of this chapter focusing on the first one.

## Compassion focused therapy

Compassion focused therapy (CFT) was developed by Professor Paul Gilbert in order to work with those suffering from high levels of shame and self-condemnation.[8] It grew out of CBT, but is also rooted in a whole range of other theories including attachment theory, neuroscience and evolutionary social psychology.[9]

Compassion focused theory is based on the fact that we are social, relational beings who are designed and motivated to live in groups.[10] From this perspective, Paul Gilbert and others have argued that shame develops when we face the threat of not being able to live within, and fully belong to, the group that is our social/care giving group.[11]

### Threat and the brain's alarm system

Gilbert's compassion focused therapy is based on the assumption that we have basic needs programmed into our human brains to cope with threat or survival. These include the need for warmth, territory, food and reproduction. In common with many animals, we have a 'threat focused brain' – a brain that is programmed to respond to threat in order to survive.[12] God has designed each one of us in this incredibly detailed way.

It is helpful at this stage to look at the response a person makes to threat in more detail, and in particular to consider the roles the amygdala and hippocampus in the brain potentially play in our response to memories of shameful events.

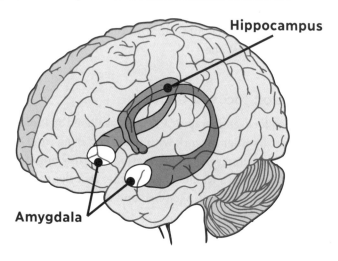

The amygdala is an almond-shaped set of neurons located in the limbic system of the brain. It is involved in the processing and regulating of emotions and storing of memories, and is highly sensitive to any threat, hence it is often referred to as the 'brain's alarm system'.[13] We have a number of responses that are automatically activated by the amygdala in order to protect us from threat. These fight/flight/freeze/submit responses are our body's automatic built-in system designed to protect us from potential danger. When we are faced with a perceived threat, the amygdala automatically tells the adrenal glands to release adrenaline in our bodies that will either help us to fight the threat or run away from it. We experience a state of high alert, as our hormones are pumping through our bodies and we are breathing faster. But we have two other automatic and instinctive responses: freeze or submit. If our brain believes we will not be able to escape, it will drop us into a 'freeze' response – one in which we literally cannot move because our heart rate and breathing have been slowed right down. From there, we may be moved into 'submit' mode, where the energy in our body is lowered even further and our thinking brain shuts off.

These instinctive and automatic responses set off by the amygdala prepare the body to cope with a physical threat and/or potentially life-threatening situation. All of this happens in a microsecond, without the person being consciously aware of all of the processes that have kicked in.

The hippocampus also forms an important part of the limbic system and is involved in regulating emotions and storing memories. It's helpful to visualise the hippocampus as a number of filing cabinets of memories in the brain. One 'filing cabinet' holds 'normal' memories that have generally been processed and are easily remembered. However, another 'filing cabinet' stores traumatic memories of events that we frequently don't want to think about because they are frightening, painful and/or shameful. In this 'filing cabinet' the memories can remain unprocessed because they are so distressing to remember that we try to avoid thinking of them.

When a person experiences a difficult event in adult life, often linked to memories of a difficult or traumatic event in childhood (including memories of when the person felt shamed or humiliated), the amygdala immediately senses a threat and reacts in the same way as though an actual physical threat is present. Memories of past shameful events flood out of the unprocessed 'filing cabinet', causing the person further distress and physical reactions.

This is a very simple explanation of a very complex process, but it's really valuable to get a grasp of this because it helps us understand what Paul Gilbert is essentially arguing in CFT: that shame is much more than a feeling. It is a self-conscious and threat-based emotion, often triggered when we feel we are facing a 'social threat' of being rejected or excluded by a group.[14]

Let's look at social pain and its effects in more detail through a hypothetical example of a thunderstorm and how three young boys, who are each playing out in the park with their mothers at the time, respond to it.

### John
We've called the first boy John. He sees the thunder and lightning and begins to feel afraid, but his mum's response is to soothe him by saying things like: 'It's OK, it's only a thunderstorm and I am here. It can't hurt you. Let's go home – we can get dry, snuggle up and have a hot chocolate together.' The result is that John begins to calm down. He has been soothed by his mum and feels accepted and affirmed, so he accepts her explanation and goes home happily. This is an important lesson that, if continued to be applied, will help him learn to self-soothe and accept himself throughout childhood and into adulthood.

## James

James has been happily playing on his own in the park while his mum chats to a friend on the phone. When the thunder and lightning strikes, however, he runs up to her, afraid. His mother's response is to impatiently tell him to grow up – she's far more interested in her conversation than in helping him to feel better. James becomes overwhelmed by his feelings, getting so angry that he hits a tree in frustration. It is possible that James may end up with an anger issue in adult life and struggle to accept himself, but may not recognise any connection to his early childhood experience. He may also become highly self-critical, full of shame and desperate for approval and affirmation. This could cause him to become driven to achieve and succeed in order to be noticed.

## Jeremy

Jeremy doesn't even really get a chance to respond to the thunder and lightning, as his mum immediately screams and says: 'Oh no! A thunderstorm, I can't stand it!' She whisks him home quickly, but does nothing to help calm him down as she's too busy panicking herself. If Jeremy continues to be ignored in such situations he may well take on his mother's behaviour, becoming highly anxious in adult life. This could lead to him turning to substances such as drink and drugs to dampen and soothe his feelings.

We will revisit John, James and Jeremy in the next chapter.

## Physical and social pain

To further consider how the brain responds to social exclusion, some very interesting research undertaken by social psychologists has demonstrated that the same area of the brain that experiences physical pain is activated by social pain such as rejection, shame etc.

MRI scans were used to scan participants while they were playing a ball game together and then, at one point, they became excluded. The same participants were also subjected to physical pain. The scans demonstrated that their brains responded to the rejection and shame in the same way as when they experienced physical pain.[15]

## Reflection

Shame is a threat-learned response. It is not a core belief; rather it is a self-conscious emotion – a threat-focused mindset. We each have our own individual physical and psychological response to shame.

In adult life, any situation that reminds a person of early childhood experiences will trigger an automatic response. It happens in a microsecond, and generally out of conscious awareness of the person. No one taught James, Jeremy and John how to cope in childhood; they just learnt how to. Once adults, when the threat of shame comes in, the same triggers kick in – and they will often respond as they did when they were children.

Does what you have learnt in this chapter help you understand your own behaviour when faced with the threat of shame? What about the behaviour of those around you too?

## Activity

In order to fully consider this notion of threat we'd like you to engage with this activity. You will need to read through the exercise first, as much of it is done with your eyes closed.

Get into a comfortable position and relax your body. Now think for a moment of someone that might be thinking of you today – perhaps wondering what you are doing, or simply thinking of you with love. Close your eyes and think about them.

Keeping your eyes closed, just begin to notice how you feel in your body. (As a guide, people often feel quite peaceful or describe feeling calm.)

Now relax just a little more deeply, keep your eyes closed and think about something that you are deeply ashamed of; something you really wouldn't want anyone to know about. Just imagine what would happen if you were asked to share information about that with a whole group of people. What response do you immediately notice in your body? (People usually describe feeling fear, anxiety, anger, palpitations, a knot in their stomach.)

While there wasn't a physical threat, your body acted as though there was. Fear often drives this. What may you have been frightened about? People often suggest that they are worried people will think less of them, or will think they are a bad person. The fear is about who you fundamentally are as a person and how you are being perceived.

This exercise is a helpful way of showing that when we face a social threat – a fear about what others will think of us – it affects us physically.

## Prayer

*Lord, I thank You that we are each marvellously and wonderfully made, in a way that encourages us to seek out beneficial relationships with one another. It is also amazing that You wired our brains to respond to threat. I thank You too for the work that psychologists, doctors and scientists have done in understanding how You have created us to be. Please help me to continue to be open to the revelation that You are giving me about my own behaviour and triggers, and of those around me whom I may help now or in the future. Amen.*

CHAPTER 4

# Strategies for dealing with shame: 1

We have seen that we have an automatic response when faced with the threat of shame, and that it is shaped by our experiences in childhood. We will now look at some strategies for helping ourselves, or others, with shame.

## Learning to self-soothe

The first thing to recognise is that individuals with high levels of shame have a range of responses they utilise to cope with the painful feelings (as we saw with the example of the three boys in the previous chapter). Paul Gilbert suggests that we need to learn how to move from these strategies to a self-soothing response.[1] He proposes that each of us has three ways or systems for regulating (coping with) the painful emotion of shame (see diagram overleaf). These systems co-ordinate our behaviour and emotions.[2]

In Gilbert's diagram, the red zone is the threat and self-protection system. In order to cope with shame and the possible threat of rejection, which is the social threat of shame, a person will focus on the threat in order to try to deal with the painful feelings.[3] So, in this zone, the person often experiences intense feelings of self-disgust, self-hate and may have anger issues, both towards others and themselves. In addition, they will frequently tell themselves that they are rubbish and worthless.

A person in this zone will also frequently isolate themselves, on the basis that they think no one would want to spend time with them. In order to deal with these extremely painful thoughts and feelings and to protect themselves, a person in the red zone will frequently focus on the threat and adopt strategies in order to 'dampen' down the emotional pain that they are feeling; for example, by making use of drugs, alcohol, food etc.[4]

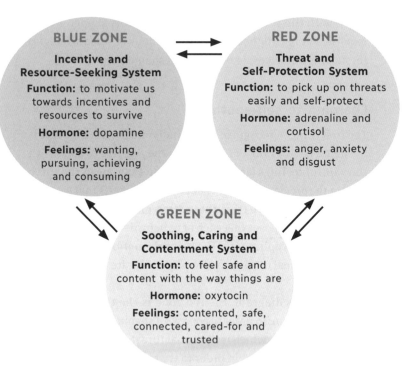

**BLUE ZONE**

**Incentive and Resource-Seeking System**

**Function:** to motivate us towards incentives and resources to survive

**Hormone:** dopamine

**Feelings:** wanting, pursuing, achieving and consuming

**RED ZONE**

**Threat and Self-Protection System**

**Function:** to pick up on threats easily and self-protect

**Hormone:** adrenaline and cortisol

**Feelings:** anger, anxiety and disgust

**GREEN ZONE**

**Soothing, Caring and Contentment System**

**Function:** to feel safe and content with the way things are

**Hormone:** oxytocin

**Feelings:** contented, safe, connected, cared-for and trusted

The blue zone is a second way a person deals with the emotions surrounding shame and is known as the 'incentive and resource-seeking system'.[5] It is still self-protecting and again a way of coping with the deep feelings of shame and fear of rejection, but this approach directs thinking to action.[6] It looks to things that are rewarding, such as money, status or achieving. People who operate in this zone are often highly driven and may be perfectionists. They strive for success and achievement and the feelings those things bring.[7] Sadly, in many ways, the competitive society in which we live fosters this by encouraging the 'need to succeed'.

People who operate in this zone often come from 'high-flyer' families. Being so energised and driven often leads to success, which helps combat the painful feelings of shame. But this approach doesn't lead to a peaceful and calm life. Interestingly, in the blue zone there is a link to a dopamine effect.

Dopamine plays a major role in the brain system. It is a neurotransmitter, which means it is responsible for transmitting signals between the brain's neurons. For example, it is used when the brain is telling the muscles of the body to move. It improves the pumping strength of the heart and blood flow to the kidneys. It also has a role in making us feel good and teaching us about behaviour by being alert to rewards and reinforcement (things we enjoy, and telling us to do the same thing again so we can get more).

Highly addictive drugs, such as cocaine, can give the same sort of effect, which is why people seek out more of them even though they are harmful. But people who are highly driven can achieve the same effect. They experience a 'high' by being excited by their success. This can be enjoyable in the short term but very unhelpful and potentially damaging in the long term.

There has been some fascinating research conducted on pastors and others in Christian ministry,[8] where findings indicated that they are often highly driven, highly motivated, activating people. This suggests they may be operating in the blue zone. On the surface this may look to be an effective strategy (and helps to deal with shame and the need to belong), but people in the blue zone are often highly self-critical and cope by busying themselves. Sadly this can lead to burnout, as being kind to themselves is a 'foreign language'.

The problem with both the red zone and the blue drive system is that the feelings don't last. This means that a person may strive more and more to succeed as behaviour becomes addictive (blue zone), or binge eat or drink (red zone), but any initial positive feelings will fade away. They certainly don't lead to a calm and peaceful mind and body.

The third zone – green – is a soothing, caring and contentment system, however. It creates a calm, soothed mind that is at rest and at peace with itself.[9] The release of oxytocin is affiliated with being in this zone. Oxytocin is a hormone that is sometimes called a 'love hormone' because it has been found that when individuals hug a loved one, their oxytocin levels increase. It is therefore associated with trust, empathy and building relationships with others. It also appears to lower stress responses.[10]

Unlike the first two zones, there isn't an emphasis on threat or achievement; instead its focus is on self-soothing, finding peace and safeness. People who naturally operate in this zone without help from counsellors will have generally been taught in childhood by their early care givers how to deal with social threat well. When there has been a physical or social threat, they have learnt from their parents that they are still acceptable and lovable. This means that, even when faced with a social threat, they are able to self-soothe and offer compassion to themselves.[11] On the other hand, children with difficult childhoods can really struggle to access this self-soothing zone.[12]

To summarise, the three circles in Gilbert's diagram represent three different responses to threat. It is important to highlight that people with shame often aren't aware of the zone they are operating in; they have just found a way to deal with the emotional pain of shame. Their strategies are instinctive and generally operate outside conscious awareness. It's probably also worth mentioning that we are unique and individual human beings, and that people often don't fit 'neatly' into one zone or another but can straddle two or maybe even three! But, generally, when there are issues of shame, a person will gravitate either towards the red or the blue zone.

To ground this in an example, let's go back to the three boys we introduced in the last chapter.

**John**

No one told John how to self-soothe when faced with threat. He simply watched and learned from his mum. Because she reminded him that he was loved and accepted, and made time to take him out of the threatening situation, over time he learned how to cope with both physical and social threat. Generally speaking, John has learned to live in the green zone. He is kind to himself, close to others and relaxed. He has a peaceful mind and body and, if he is a Christian, he may well be able to connect more easily with God.

**James**

No one told James that if he becomes angry he will feel as though he is staying safe and it will help him to cope.

It is simply a learned behaviour in response to his mum ignoring him. He also may end up as a highly driven person, which moves him into the blue zone. As he was ignored in the past, he has no intention of being ignored now so he is driven to succeed and be noticed – achieving becomes his passion.

**Jeremy**
No one told Jeremy to be highly anxious when faced with threat. He simply observed and learned from his mum. Insecurely attached, anxious children become focused on anxiety and fear, thinking about dangers all the time, as a way of trying to cope with the fear. So, as an adult, he might be a person who stays in the red zone. Perhaps he learned to shut himself off from others. He may have become addicted to alcohol or another substance because he hasn't learned to self-soothe in any other way. He hates himself and hates how he is but can't stop. Being kind to himself is totally foreign – it actually seems quite frightening.

## Understanding our instinctive responses

Understanding where a person's instinctive responses to shame and the threat of rejection come from is vital. As we have already said, in some counselling and pastoral care approaches it was thought that merely allowing the client to tell their story of shame was enough for them to process it and 'move on'. Now we know more about how the human brain processes threat, we understand we need more than that. Nevertheless, understanding someone's childhood is going to be very important, as so many of our automated responses develop then.

Whether it is yourself or someone else you are helping, it is really important to explore whether the person feels able to share painful memories. Creating a safe space will be vital in aiding this. (Make sure you stop and simply care for the person if they become upset.) Here are some useful questions to ask:

1. What were your biggest fears in childhood?
2. What strategies did you develop in order to cope with them?
3. What were the most painful and shameful events in your childhood?
4. What did you think other people were thinking about you at the time?
5. What were the kind of things you said to yourself during difficult times?

As you explore the coping strategies and the feelings the person had (whether yourself or someone else), it is important to confirm that you understand why they developed these ways of coping. They might not be the best ways of coping and thinking in the here and now but, as a child, they were probably the only ways they could find to cope.

What you are trying to do, as per Gilbert's theory and diagram, is to help someone move from the red or blue zone to the green zone. Heather has found that giving out Gilbert's diagram to her clients can be helpful. For example, there have been many who have had a lightbulb moment as they've identified which circle they are operating in. This is the first step to being able to stop the unhealthy cycle of response, because understanding the why behind the way we think and act is a huge part of being able to make changes.

Judy had been sexually abused as a child and, for as long as she could remember, had always used food as a way to comfort herself. She went to therapy because she was desperate to break this habit and lose weight. Heather and Judy explored the blocks to her eating more normally and healthily, but whenever they discussed ways she might want to stop overeating, a part of Judy screamed: 'No one is going to tell me what to do.' Heather helped Judy understand that in childhood, in order to deal with the abuse, she developed a strategy that no one was ever again going to tell her what to do. In part, this was very helpful, because it stopped her being abused again. But, in adult life, it also impeded her joining weight loss groups as she viewed them as 'being told what to eat'. It also interfered with her trying to regain some control over her eating. Helping Judy realise how much her childhood was impacting her present, and understanding where that inner script came from, helped her to move towards a more gentle and self-compassionate response to herself. It also helped Judy find other ways to 'soothe' herself, without the use of food.

## Reflection

We have seen that each one of us has an instinctive response to shame and the threat of rejection, but that learning to be compassionate to ourselves is an important way to break the cycle of unhelpful responses. If we weren't taught how to do this or we never saw it modelled in childhood, then we will find it more difficult to learn as an adult. The kindness, love and empathy that we all need from others and from ourselves are what a loving family should have given to us in childhood. Those of us that didn't have that will find it more difficult, but not impossible, to care for ourselves well. The first step is recognising where we are at.

## Activity

We will pick up how to help ourselves and others operate in the green zone in later chapters. For now, understanding our own responses to threat, and what would help us move more towards the green zone, is incredibly helpful. In this activity, you are going to think about those you may have helped who are facing a lot of shame, as well as how you can help yourself.

Think about a friend or someone you have helped in pastoral care. As a result of their shame, which circle/zone do you think they were operating in? How do you know? (In other words, what was the behaviour that led you to this conclusion?)

Having read about the different responses to the threat of shame, how might you have been different with them?

And what about yourself? Can you pinpoint which circle/ zone you have a tendency to operate out of? How does that help you understand your response to threat?

It is important to note that sometimes we can operate out of more than one circle/zone. It can also be difficult to discern what is God-given, healthy ambition, and what leads into unhealthy habits. Think about what the deep-level motivation for your actions is, as this can be a real clue. Doing something because you are motivated by shame is not healthy.

What is it that would help you move into the green zone and be more kind to yourself?

## Prayer

*Lord, it is so interesting to see the links between our childhood responses to threat and how we live our lives as adults. Help me to truly understand my own instinctive responses, as well as those of the people around me whom You have brought into my life for me to help and support. I don't want to live unhealthily, so I ask for Your help to transform my wrong thinking and self-destructive habits. Help me to build positive, healthy habits in my life and in my thinking to know Your compassion and love for me. Amen.*

CHAPTER 5

# Strategies for dealing with shame: 2

Having looked at Gilbert's compassion focused approach, we are now going to review some of the work of Janina Fisher, which seems to build on what we have learnt so far.

## Understanding the 'parts of self'

Another way of looking at what happens to us when we are under threat is to recognise that when events in adult life occur that are similar to those that gave rise to the feelings of shame in childhood, different 'parts of self' are likely to emerge. This simply means that, when a person experiences stress or trauma in adult life, a child part, which holds the trauma and shame of childhood, can emerge.[1] An adult part of self will see things quite rationally, but a child part will feel and experience the intense emotional pain and shame.

Heather has found the work of Janina Fisher, an expert in working with trauma survivors, extremely helpful because, like Gilbert, Fisher also considers how to help a client regulate their emotions and soothe the shame part.[2]

Fisher provides a very helpful diagram in her book *Healing the Fragmented Selves of Trauma Survivors* (2017), and we will use a simplified version to further explain this concept.[3]

To go back to the fight/flight/freeze/submit responses mentioned earlier, when an adult faces an event that reminds them of some shameful events in childhood (even if this occurs outside conscious awareness), overwhelming feelings come flooding back in an instant – and the childhood strategies kick in.

As you can see from the diagram, the adult part of the brain (Fisher calls it the 'going on with normal life part of the self'),[4] goes offline and its influence reduces, leaving the 'trauma-related part of the personality' (in other words, the child part holding the shame and trauma) to immediately become activated.[5]

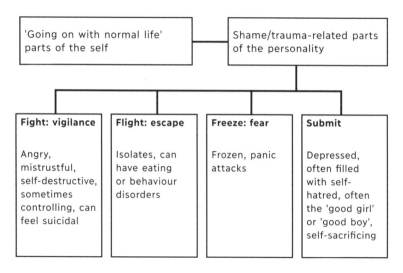

| 'Going on with normal life' parts of the self | Shame/trauma-related parts of the personality | | |
|---|---|---|---|
| **Fight: vigilance** | **Flight: escape** | **Freeze: fear** | **Submit** |
| Angry, mistrustful, self-destructive, sometimes controlling, can feel suicidal | Isolates, can have eating or behaviour disorders | Frozen, panic attacks | Depressed, often filled with self-hatred, often the 'good girl' or 'good boy', self-sacrificing |

This process happens in a split second and kicks in instinctively.[6] Fisher argues that to treat shame, we have to 'wake up' the thinking (adult) part of the brain again to help it come back online and come to the fore.[7] To achieve this, Fisher asserts that it can be helpful for a person to adopt the practice of mindfulness in order to take a mindful approach.[8]

## Mindfulness

In 1979, molecular biologist Jon Kabat Zinn opened a clinic to teach meditation and mindfulness to patients struggling with all sorts of problems including depression, anxiety and even cancer diagnoses. He drew on 2,500 years of mindfulness teaching from Zen Buddhism to create a stress reduction programme, teaching his patients about the importance of stepping out of what they were experiencing.[9] This helped them to understand that the thoughts and feelings are *just* thoughts and feelings, so we are able to let them go. He focused on getting patients to pay attention to the present moment without judging (or rejecting) it and to have an attitude of curiosity, openness and acceptance.

Therapists started to become very interested as to how mindfulness might be used in therapy. Today, it has been integrated into much therapy and counselling.

Some Christians are concerned about mindfulness, due to its origins in Buddhism. However, what has been imported into western psychotherapy is not Buddhist. It is simply focused on helping someone accept painful or difficult emotional experiences, rather than trying to get rid of them. While CBT can be about monitoring and reviewing thoughts and emotions, looking at evidence that may or may not support the thoughts and exploring and facilitating change in behaviour, mindfulness encourages people to simply become more aware of their thoughts and feelings; to be accepting, not necessarily engaging with the thoughts, but being able to tolerate some discomfort as they stay in the present moment.

Many Christians practise mindfulness, believing that an emphasis on being in the present moment is something that Jesus taught.[10] We can certainly see this in His teaching on worry. In Matthew 6:34, for instance, He encourages the disciples to: 'Give your entire attention to what God is doing right now, and don't get worked up about what may or may not happen tomorrow. God will help you deal with whatever hard things come up when the time comes' (*The Message*).

We also see the psalmists being mindful when they describe their current emotions without judgment. They simply accept where they are, but then speak rational truth over themselves. For example, true anguish is described in Psalm 42:3,5: 'My tears have been my food day and night... Why, my soul, are you downcast? Why so disturbed within me? Put your hope in God, for I will yet praise him, my Saviour and my God.'

They don't try to hide their anguish, but recognise that hoping and praising God will help.

Claire first came across mindfulness when working on previous titles in the *Insight* series; then there came a spate of Christian mindfulness books. Rather than jumping on what seemed to be a new fad among Christian writers, Claire approached mindfulness with caution. However, she has come to see that becoming more aware and attentive to the present moment is something that traditional Christian meditation helps with. It can also open us up to more of God's creativity (think of Psa. 143:5, where it says: 'I meditate on all your works and consider what your hands have done'). Claire has found that using mindfulness to simply slow down and be 'in the moment' before God has helped to create a sense of calm and peace each morning before she starts work.

## Dealing with the child part

If we are trying to encourage ourselves or someone else to move from the blue/red zones and into the green zone, which we looked at previously, utilising a mindful approach can be very helpful because it helps a person step back to notice and observe their emotions, rather than being overwhelmed by them.[11] Fisher acknowledges that mindfulness helps people to slow down both their thoughts and feelings as well as their physical reactions. They are able to become more aware of both the adult and child parts and what they are saying.[12] Research has demonstrated the effectiveness of mindfulness in assisting individuals to slow down, pause and deal with their emotional responses.[13] This helps to activate the left (adult) part of the brain, which automatically kicks in a self-soothing response. This has therefore become an important process within compassion focused therapy too. People are taught to be non-judgmental: to simply be curious, observe their body and emotional reactions and be in the present moment.

Here is a suggestion of how we can use this approach to help ourselves or someone else be more mindful of our/their responses.

- Help the person learn to observe overwhelming feelings and impulses. Help them notice what is happening – both in their body and in their emotions.
- Often a person will say: 'I feel such shame' or 'I hate myself'. While this is experienced as all-encompassing, reflect it back by saying: 'So a part of you feels shame – tell me a little more about that part.'
- Ask them what they do when that part gets upset and help them identify their response. (Do utilise Fisher's diagram

if it would be helpful, in order to point out the fight/flight/freeze/submit responses. Heather finds it helpful to hand the diagram out to clients and has found that many have immediately identified their child part and the corresponding strategy.)

- Once identified, help the person not to judge the response that part has. Affirm that it was the survival part and the strategy that went with it that got them through childhood.
- Try to identify the trigger. What is it that activates that part and causes the thinking part to go offline?
- It is helpful to ask: 'What does that child part need at the moment?' Reassure the child part that you are listening to them and that you are not going to ignore them.
- Try to help the adult part to negotiate with the child part (as a good parent would do to a child – in many ways you are modelling this by listening to the child part). Ask how the adult part wants to respond to the child part. What would it want to say? (You are trying to create a dialogue between the parts.) Don't worry if it goes pear-shaped – the adult part could say 'I hate her' and the child part go quiet! However, if you continue to respond compassionately to both parts, your response will be healing to the person.
- Another question that can be useful to ask is: 'How can we be compassionate to the child part?' An adult part may well struggle with this, so you could use imagery and say, 'If a little girl or boy was saying this, what would you say to them?' Or, 'How would you help a young adult you love?' So many of us are incredibly compassionate to others but not towards ourselves. Helping a person find their compassionate part and apply it to themselves is so helpful. You can use the imagination to get them to remember the last time they felt

compassionate to another person. Get them to describe how they felt and what they said. Ultimately, it's about both parts working together and accepting each other.

As we are helping someone else, or ourselves, we are being God's hand and feet to them. Just think of how compassionate Jesus was to those He met and ministered to. When the leper in Matthew 8:1–3 approached Him, Jesus immediately reached out His hand and touched him. That would have been the one thing that the leper had not experienced since contracting leprosy, as everyone else would have been scared to touch him. The feelings of isolation and rejection, as society shunned lepers at the time, would have been immense. Jesus met those head-on with such a compassionate action, which went to the heart of the leper's shame.

- Once the child part has been acknowledged and listened to, you might want to get them to consider the strategy that that part uses and think about whether it is helpful. You might need to say: 'Does that part need to dictate to you the outcome of your life? While you can still give lots of love to that part, what is it stopping you doing?' The child part had found a way to survive. But in adult life, that survival strategy can be the very thing that blocks us from doing what we want to achieve, or it blocks us from finding freedom and being who God made us to be. We will revisit this theme in the following chapters.

*A word of caution*

It may be that someone simply needs empathy and kindness – they may not be at a place to recognise the different parts. Someone deeply depressed, or highly traumatised for instance, would probably not be able to work through this process and simply providing compassion and listening will be the most helpful response, rather than trying to force the issue.

To show how helpful this approach can be, here is how Heather used it when working with Sylvia. She was an incredibly successful businesswoman but had learned as a child (and had had the message reinforced in the business world) that she should never show weakness, never cry and never rely on anyone else. She went to Heather with the goal of being able to cry. Using counselling techniques and the theories described above, Heather worked patiently and methodically with her, helping Sylvia understand that as a result of an abusive childhood, her child part had learned it was not safe to cry. Her child part went into 'fight' mode as soon as any social threat appeared, and became hypervigilant. It took two years, but eventually Sylvia was able to cry.

Heather was also able to utilise this approach to work through a very painful memory of her own. When she was 11, she took the 11+ exam but failed it. Her mum went around telling everyone, within her earshot, that she had passed. Somehow that gave Heather the message that she was beyond not being good enough – that she was such a failure her mum had to lie about her. She took into adulthood the idea that she mustn't fail, learning to only do things that she knew she would succeed at. That is not helpful when God calls you to do something that takes you out of your comfort zone! Fairly recently, while she was preparing for a talk, her boss casually remarked that he would be going along to the event and was looking forward to hearing her speak. Heather is used to public speaking, but when he mentioned he would be going, the 'child' part immediately kicked in and all of the old feelings of shame surfaced again. She was able to recognise that child part, took time to talk to herself in a soothing manner, and prayed that God would help her relax and focus on the day, which is exactly what happened.

## Reflection

We have looked in this chapter at how the responses we had as a child can be triggered in adulthood when we face the threat of shame, and yet they can stop us from being all that we can be. Understanding how the different parts of ourselves can come 'online' can help us to be more aware of our subconscious behaviour. Learning to be soothing and compassionate to ourselves is a vital step in activating change, to help us move towards the place of peace that God longs for us to be able to operate from.

## Activity

Take some time to think over the theories from Gilbert and Fisher that we have covered in this and the previous chapter. Can you see how they would be helpful when helping others deal with shame? How about yourself?

## Prayer

*Lord, I thank You that You have given us each a capacity to be compassionate. Help me to be compassionate not only to those You bring into my path to help, but also myself. Help me also to be more aware of the moment that I am in. Rather than dwelling on the past or worrying about the future, I pray I can be fully present in today and be aware of all that You have for me. Amen.*

CHAPTER 6

# Repairing the wounds of the past: 1

We have seen how the same responses we had to trauma/shame as children are often triggered in adulthood. While we have looked at some strategies for recognising and soothing our response, as Christians we believe that God can bring healing to difficult situations and circumstances from the past that have wounded us. The rest of this book will be focused on what we can do to find further healing from shame, and also how we can bring more of our faith into the process of dealing with, and letting go of, past shame.

## The Waverley Integrative Framework

To understand more fully the effect that shame can have on us, it is helpful to consider how we are whole people made up of five areas of functioning (see the Waverley Integrative Framework, Appendix 1). We are all physical beings who experience emotions and have choices about how we behave. We have the ability to think things through, and we are spiritual beings. Therefore, when shame is triggered within us, it will affect every part of our beings, including the spiritual. (We have already seen how shame can directly affect our thinking and that we can have a physical response to it too.) Here is a brief summary of the five areas of our being:

- Emotional – this is the area that covers our feelings. Often these can signal where our difficulties lie.
- Behavioural – this area makes the connection between what we are thinking and the goals we choose to set ourselves. So it is about the choices we make, albeit choices sometimes made outside our conscious awareness, including the way we behave.
- Cognitive – this refers to everything involved in our thinking selves, such as specific thoughts, beliefs, values and plans.
- Physical – we are all physical beings, but how healthy our bodies are is not just down to illness and injuries that we may pick up, but also the effect of all other areas of our functioning as humans. Sometimes our emotional state or belief pattern can affect us physically – but also physical dysfunction such as illness, a lack of sleep or unhealthy diet can impact our sense of spiritual wellbeing too.
- Spiritual – our inner core, where our deepest longings and thirsts are located.

It says in 1 Thessalonians 5:23: 'May your whole spirit, soul and body be kept blameless at the coming of our Lord Jesus Christ.' This is a great, broad picture of how each of us is made. The Waverley Integrative Framework (initially formulated by Selwyn Hughes who founded CWR, and previously known as the Waverley Model) is based on this, and can be described as an integrative approach that views a person as being inherently relational, designed by God to be in relationship with Him and others. It is also a holistic approach that views a person as having the above core aspects of human functioning: emotional, behavioural, cognitive, physical and spiritual.

This holistic understanding of human nature helps us to

understand how we work. If one part of us is not healthy then it will affect everything else. It is just like an apple that you cut open only to find that it's going bad in the middle. If you had left that apple a bit longer, it would have started going bad all the way through. This is a good demonstration of what can happen to the different aspects of our lives. For instance, if you are struggling with your emotions then it can affect the way you are thinking and feeling, which can then have a knock-on effect on your behaviour.

When shame is triggered in us, all five areas of functioning are usually affected. We may sense a change in our body: tension in our stomach, a rising pulse, clammy hands, and then negative emotions become aroused. Our thoughts will also begin to change and may become distorted, and we may start feeling the need to fight or choose to run away and hide. Try the activity below to see how shame can affect your whole self.

## Activity

Think of a time when you faced a situation where memories of past shameful events were triggered. What areas of your human functioning were affected during it? Look again at the Waverley Integrative Framework to help you with this, and also try to pinpoint exactly how you felt in that situation. In your mind, put yourself back there and consider: What emotions am I experiencing? How am I behaving? What thoughts are going through my mind? Am I feeling physically sick? Is my heart racing? Am I feeling stressed? How am I affected spiritually? Is my sense of self being affected? (This is a helpful exercise to do with someone else too, particularly if they are struggling to see how much a past event is still affecting them.)

## Emotional

As we have discussed, a variety of emotions accompany shame. To find healing from shame, the shame has to be challenged, but it has to be done in such a way that it doesn't reinforce the emotions of shame. While we have said that just vocalising the story of shame doesn't go far enough, it is important that we don't neglect this and do allow ourselves or others to go through the process of talking about memories. Being kind and listening to someone as they do so, or giving ourselves the space to think and speak it out, helps the person to move away from the stress response. It causes the person to relax and learn to be kind to themselves, to be less self-critical, and to self-soothe in helpful ways. As Gilbert's theory suggests, this helps a person to move towards the green zone, where minds are calm.

Some people are fearful of compassion and acceptance – whether self-compassion, or compassion shown by another. Sometimes this is due to being concerned that they will become weak or unable to cope themselves (they believe they can't let their guard down).[1] But actually, as we've seen, when they are able to become more compassionate towards themselves they become more relaxed and stronger as they move towards the green zone.

If someone you are helping finds compassion and kindness difficult to accept, you might want to ask what they think might happen if they started to be empathetic and warm towards themselves. Or perhaps what their worst fear would be if they offered themselves kindness. If you know you have a problem accepting compassion, ask yourself the same questions. As we saw earlier, Jesus showed such compassion to those He interacted with. Even those who were guilty of some wrongdoing were dealt with with kindness. Think about the woman who was caught in the act of adultery. Those around her had decided to shame just her (not the man involved – a reflection of society's views at the time), and demanded that she be stoned. What was Jesus' response? In John 8:7, He says: 'Let any one of you who is without sin be the first to throw a stone at her'. When they all left, He simply said to the woman: 'Go now and leave your life of sin' (v11). Rather than making a big deal of her sin, He confounded those who sought her execution, and then in one simple sentence offered her her life back. What love and compassion! Given that example, how do you think He would respond to you? And how do you think He would want you to respond to yourself?

When you model kindness, acceptance and compassion, whether to yourself or someone else, it cultivates an atmosphere in which unhelpful feelings can be noticed and empathy and kindness activated. This is about locating the kind part of yourself, rather than allowing the critical part to have free rein. You might suggest that the other person (or yourself) does one kind thing for themselves every day.

## BLOCKS TO SELF-COMPASSION

For a number of people, there are some blocks to being able to offer themselves self-compassion. For example, some believe that having compassion for oneself is somehow an 'easy option'. But that's not true: compassion is not an easy option as it still requires facing pain, but learning to be kind to ourselves as we do so. Look at the activity on the next page, which includes this and other myths about compassion.

## Activity

The following chart has been taken and slightly adapted from the work of clinical psychologist Deborah Lee.[2]

Take some time to work through the table below, which challenges various myths about compassion. The first two have been done for you – try and fill in the rest yourself.

| Myths about compassion | Compassionate reason why this is a myth |
|---|---|
| Compassion is OK for others, but it's not OK for me – I don't deserve it. | This is a double standard. I deserve compassion just as much as everyone else. |
| Compassion is the easy option. | Compassion is not easy – it takes immense bravery to face past pain and offer compassion to myself. |
| Compassion is like wallowing in self-pity; it's selfish. | |
| Showing compassion to myself will make me weak. | |
| Compassion is fluffy, airy-fairy stuff. | |

| | |
|---|---|
| Having compassion for myself makes me vulnerable to others. | |
| Being compassionate means I cannot be angry. | |
| Being compassionate lets me off the hook. | |

## Behavioural

As we have already seen, one of the ways in which shame affects our behaviour is the strong desire to run away that it creates. Many people who experience shame say to themselves: 'Why would people want to know me?' (From a rational perspective, this is obviously a wrong belief/thought, but at a heart level is firmly believed. This gives evidence of how inter-connected the different areas of our beings are.) The thought plays on their mind and causes them to take action by going into hiding.

This reflects the Genesis creation account that we looked at earlier, when Adam and Eve's immediate response was to go and find some way to cover themselves, and then to hide from God. However, the deep consequence of such behaviour is that people become intensely lonely. Often, those trapped in a cycle of unhelpful responses to shame are crying out for love, attention and acceptance from others, but they simply aren't able to reach out. God created each of us with an inbuilt need for acceptance and love, so hiding from others has a detrimental effect on our wellbeing.

In helping yourself or another person dealing with shame, finding a network of relationships or a support system is really important. Relationships encourage healing, even if they take effort to begin with (as the person has to overcome their intense desire to hide). Apart from anything else, research has shown the importance of emotional connection with others for reducing stress levels, which leads to significant mental health and physical health benefits.[3] This could be why groups like Alcoholics Anonymous have had so much success, because the shame of alcohol addiction is dealt with in a group where everyone accepts each other. When we are loved and accepted we learn and start to believe that we are lovable, which is why it is so important to encourage ourselves and others to connect with other people. It might be helpful to refer back to Gilbert's diagram and think about unhealthy behavioural strategies used to cope with shame, and then to consider more helpful, soothing ones. It can be so useful for us to share those things with others too. For example, we could let them know what it is that helps us when we are struggling, so that they are well prepared for when we do need their help.

We might also need to help others, or ourselves, to take responsibility for any self-damaging behaviour. Perhaps they (or we) are working too hard or drinking – it is important to slow down and take stock of the potential impact that might be having. The key is recognising the unhelpful strategies or behaviours that have been adopted in response to past shameful events. Then we can begin to take baby steps to try to change our behaviour, and adopt more helpful and healthy ways of looking after ourselves.

A SAFE PLACE

When we are finding our behaviour is being affected by shame (and perhaps becoming distressed), it can be helpful to visualise a 'safe place'. Heather first came across this suggestion in Lee's work.[4] This safe place could be an actual place previously visited, or it could be an imaginary place. Whichever it is, when a person feels they are becoming distressed, they can visualise taking themselves to this place. The visualisation below will help with the self-soothing process.

---

## Activity

To help you or someone else create a safe place, work through this visualisation:

Find a peaceful, calm place to sit and relax yourself into a chair, focusing on your breathing and taking time to relax each muscle.

Close your eyes and begin to think about the environment in which you feel completely safe. The following questions may help you to visualise it:

- What does it look like?
- Is it inside or outside?
- What does it smell like?
- What do you like doing there?

Once you have fully visualised it, take some time to simply 'be' within that space, allowing yourself the time to fully relax.

Heather had a Christian client, Susan, who disclosed at the beginning of therapy that she often drank too much. As they began to work together, Heather discovered that Susan believed that God disliked her and was going to punish her in some way. Having explored childhood events and discovered where these beliefs came from, Heather suggested that creating a safe place could help her to combat this, particularly when she was beginning to feel troubled. Susan learned to put on worship music and go to that safe place, and found it extremely helpful. She also addressed her difficulties with alcohol and, while overcoming this was tough, by starting to value herself and be compassionate towards herself, over time Susan was able to stop drinking.

## Cognitive

When someone is suffering from shame, it is as though a self-critical message is on a loop, playing round and round in their head. They will focus on what they believe is wrong with them, and this will cause them to believe that they are fundamentally bad, worthless and unlovable. They believe this is how others think of them too. When shame is deeply internalised, almost nothing about themselves is believed to be OK.[5]

People with high shame will also have difficulty accepting – or even noticing – when people praise or compliment them. What they tend to do is focus on anything that confirms the belief that they are worthless, while ignoring anything that disproves it. But this goes against what God says about us, so these thoughts and feelings, however true and real they feel to the person at the time, cannot be the truth. So, a person with high levels of shame may often find it helpful to meditate on the fact that they are God's beloved child (see Rom. 8:17; 1 John 3:1), accepted and adopted by Him, and to also follow Paul's advice in Philippians 4:8 and dwell on: 'whatever is true, whatever is noble, whatever is right, whatever is pure, whatever is lovely, whatever is admirable – if anything is excellent or praiseworthy – think about such things'. This is a great reminder to take the time to dwell on the good and positive things about ourselves. However, we should also remember not to beat ourselves up when the negative thoughts *do* appear. Our God loves us unconditionally; that means He looks upon us with love and acceptance even when we are struggling with shameful thoughts!

We also believe it is worth saying that, as Christians, we can sometimes have the wrong perception that we need to have everything together constantly. Not only does this put added stress on ourselves, it also simply is not true! The Bible tells us that 'we have this treasure in jars of clay' (2 Cor. 4:7). God recognises that we are fragile, but this provides the opportunity to show Him at work in our lives (that verse goes on to say 'to show that this all-surpassing power is from God and not from us'.)

RE-SCRIPTING SHAMEFUL THOUGHTS

As we have seen, people struggling with shame tend to focus on negative thoughts. While thoughts are neutral in and of themselves, it is when we allow them to affect how we are feeling, how we are behaving and our overall sense of wellbeing that they become problematic. Again, mindfulness can help with this, as it causes us to stand back and reflect objectively on our thinking. While our minds can get caught up with self-critical thoughts, mindfulness helps us to distinguish between us as individuals and the critical thoughts so that they no longer need to control us. It also gives us time to step back, and, rather than beating ourselves up for thinking negatively, to simply recognise and accept a thought and then identify the best course of action (which could be to challenge the thought directly).

As Christians, we are told to 'be transformed by the renewing of your mind' (Rom. 12:2) and to 'take captive every thought to make it obedient to Christ' (2 Cor. 10:5). Having already said that we can't just change what is happening in our heads – our hearts need to be involved too – it is important to say that we do need to follow biblical advice, but we aren't doing this in our own strength. We can ask the Holy Spirit to help the changes reach our hearts as well as our heads. Once we've understood the why behind the shame-based thinking, we are in a better position to battle it, as we are told to in the verses above. For example, once we have identified a negative thought, we can take the time to think of a more realistic viewpoint – and even back this truth up with a scripture that we can look at regularly. If this is something you would find helpful, why not fill out the table below (the first entry is done for you as an example).

| What is my negative thought saying? | A more realistic thought | Scriptures to remind me of this truth |
|---|---|---|
| I am useless, a failure at everything I do. | I may occasionally make mistakes, but God has made me unique, with talents and gifts I can use. | 'I am fearfully and wonderfully made' (Psa. 139:14) 'we are God's handiwork, created in Christ Jesus to do good works, which God prepared in advance for us to do' (Eph. 2.10) |

| What is my negative thought saying? | A more realistic thought | Scriptures to remind me of this truth |
|---|---|---|
|  |  |  |
|  |  |  |
|  |  |  |

## Activity

If you know you find it difficult to recognise and then let go of negative thoughts, try the exercises below, which are taken from *Insight into Self-Acceptance.* [6]

### Laying our negative thoughts at the foot of the cross

1. Visualise the cross.
2. See your negative thought written on a piece of paper, and mentally hold this in the palms of your hands in front of you. Try not to evaluate or judge the thought; it is only a thought – a mental activity. If you find yourself judging it, just accept that and gently bring your mind back to holding the thought in front of you again. Your mind will automatically wander and want to make judgments, so be patient with yourself.
3. Walk up to the cross and either lay this piece of paper with your thought at the foot of the cross, or hand it over to Jesus.
4. Now walk away.

### Floating clouds

1. Repeat step 2 from the above exercise.
2. Now place that thought on a cloud and watch it drift away.
3. When another thought comes into your mind, again, without judging it, simply place it on a cloud.

(Some people find this exercise more helpful if they place the thought on a lily pad and watch it float downstream.)

### Compassionate letter writing

One of the ways that we can replace shameful scripts is by writing a letter to ourselves, as Gilbert suggests. [7] This letter should be kind and compassionate, showing empathy for what has happened rather than being critical or cold (so it should use phrases such as 'I understand why you...').

It can be difficult to write this kind of letter when we are really struggling, so it is better to wait and do this exercise when we feel we are able to engage with it well.

## Activity

To understand how to use letter writing to help someone else, or yourself, try writing one. Start by thinking of a shame memory and then consider what you would say to yourself if you were being compassionate. You might want to ask yourself the following questions to help you:

1. How can I express concern and genuine care for myself?
2. How can I be sensitive to my own needs and distress?
3. How can I write in a way that is non-judgmental?
4. How does writing with kindness make me feel?

**Perfect nurturer**

Another intervention that Heather has found useful, which was also suggested by Lee, is to help someone develop an internal 'perfect nurturer'.[8] They are encouraged to think of a person who is compassionate towards them, someone who would care for them and who would calm, soothe and reassure them.

## Activity

The following exercise has again been taken and slightly adapted from Lee's book *The Compassionate Mind Approach to Recovering from Trauma using Compassion Focused Therapy.*

In order to help yourself or someone else, take some time to think about what a kind carer would look like for you/them. The following questions may be helpful:

1. What does your perfect nurturer look like? Are they tall or short? Male or female? Young or old?
2. When you are struggling, what would you like your nurturer to say to you, and what sort of voice would you like them to use (soft, low, strong, calm)?
3. What else would you like your nurturer to offer you in terms of comfort – a hug? A cup of tea?

It is important to recognise that these exercises could activate some grief, as the person is grieving things that should never have happened in childhood. Give yourself, or the other person, some time and space to acknowledge and process this. It can be helpful to share with another trusted Christian and pray together over the grief and sadness that has surfaced. Ask God to bring you/the other person peace and comfort as you experience the grief.

In addition, as you do these exercises yourself or with another, think about what the perfect nurturer might say to the child part that is experiencing grief. This can really help a person get in touch with the compassionate part of themselves, and how they might show compassion to the child part. (You may find it helpful to visualise building a compassionate image in order to aid this. Much like the nurturer, this is an image that is non-judgmental, wise, warm etc – something that is full of compassion towards you. The difference is it doesn't have to be a person, but can be an animal or even an inanimate object. Gilbert provides an exercise on how to do this on his website, which helps you think about what the image looks and sounds like, as well as how it relates to you and you relate to it.[9])

## Reflection

Take some time to think about the five areas of functioning suggested in the Waverley Integrative Framework. How do you feel about the way that each area is interlinked with another? Can you see how the various areas are affected by one another in your own life? What do you need to be more mindful of, moving forward? Could it be how your thinking affects your emotions? Or how your emotions affect your behaviour?

## Activity

We have looked at ways to calm and soothe, as well as replace negative thinking. To end this chapter, we'd like you to take some time to really think about the fact that God is the ultimate nurturer of our whole beings. He knows us inside out (as Psalm 139 shows us, He knitted us together, knows the hairs on our heads, He knows what we like and don't like, what triggers us and what comforts us). Use one of these ideas to help you do this:

- Visualise drawing closer to God – perhaps through a passage of Scripture, by returning to your safe place and asking Him to join you, or any other way you would find helpful.
- Think about ways to describe God and the specific ways that you would like to feel His care in your life (such as 'God is a safe tower for us to run to – I would love to sense that safety more in those moments when I feel ashamed or stressed').
- Write a letter to God, thanking Him for His compassion, love and care – and anything else you would like to say to Him

(perhaps voicing some of your struggles and asking Him to help you).

---

## Prayer

*God, it is amazing to reflect on how all the different parts that make us human are interlinked. Help me to be more aware of how I am affected, in life generally as well as when I am specifically dealing with shame. I offer up my whole being to You afresh. Please help me to be guided by You, and please show me when I need to work through past shame and allow You to open up past wounds in order for them to be healed by You. I thank You for all the practical suggestions provided in this chapter; lead me to utilise the ones that will work best for me and for those You want me to help. Amen.*

CHAPTER 7

# Repairing the wounds of the past: 2

We have been looking at the different areas of functioning from the Waverley Integrative Framework, and how shame affects each of them. In this chapter, we focus on the final two: physical and spiritual.

## Physical

Shame is a powerful activator of stress responses, and we have already seen (in Chapter 3) how there is a physical impact when we feel triggered by shame. With our body responding to the shame as a threat, it puts us into high alert physically, so that we are ready to respond with 'fight', 'flight', 'freeze' or 'submit'. But being in this level of high alert when there is no physical danger can have an adverse effect on both our mental and physical health. Learning to activate the body's relaxation response is a really helpful way of calming down the physical and emotional symptoms.

When we relax, there are many beneficial ways in which our physical bodies respond: our heart rate decreases, muscles relax, blood pressure lowers and our breathing slows down. If we are living with high levels of shame, learning to kickstart the body into relaxing will be extremely helpful.

We will each have different ways to relax that we find most effective. It may be that reading, listening to (worship) music, meditating on Scripture, sewing, colouring, getting out into nature or taking a bath surrounded by candles relaxes you. Perhaps it involves spending time with friends or family. If you aren't sure what relaxes you, thinking back to what you said helped move you into the green zone (see activity at the end of Chapter 4) may provide you with some practical ways to combat the physical response to shame. As we have already seen, mindfulness is seen as a key way of helping us to soothe ourselves. Heather has found Christian mindfulness apps to be a really effective way for both herself and clients to interact with mindfulness.

Heather would describe herself as a very busy person, often rushing from one activity to another. While she is often energised by new activities (sometimes operating in the blue zone!), she can get tired and weary. She has found spending ten minutes a day using a Christian mindfulness meditation app incredibly helpful in assisting her to slow down her breathing, relax her body and most importantly connect with God, in order to experience His love and rest. In addition, relaxing and doing tapestry in the evenings has really helped her slow down and feel restored.

## SLOW BREATHING

Learning slow, controlled breathing can also be a great way of relaxing us too; if we can halt the physical symptoms of shame by breathing ourselves into a calmer state, we will then be able to look more rationally at the cause rather than getting caught up in our emotions.

The breathing exercise we introduce below has an effect upon our bodies' autonomic nervous systems. We have already talked about how our body can automatically kick into 'fight, flight, freeze or submit' mode – this is due to the sympathetic nervous system being activated. As a result, our heartbeat quickens, we breathe more quickly and adrenaline increases (when we are in this high alert mode, we tend to breathe more shallowly, which means we take in more 'in' breaths). The parasympathetic nervous system does the exact opposite, so when we breathe slowly, our heart rate slows and our blood pressure reduces. These two systems work in opposition to each other, so when one is active the other is more passive. We can actively cause our body's natural relaxation mechanism to kick in by making each 'out' breath last longer than each 'in' breath.[1]

## Activity

This exercise can be done anywhere and at any time, so it is a helpful tool for when we first notice a physical response to the threat of shame. You may want to practise the exercise daily to begin with, so that you become really familiar with it.

- Sit comfortably on a chair. You can choose to close your eyes or not – just do whatever is comfortable for you.
- Become aware that the chair is taking your body weight, and how it does that. Feel the pressure of your feet on the floor; note where your hands are and how they feel.
- Next, become aware of any noises around you, just simply noting them rather than being distracted by them.
- Then become aware of your own breathing; breathe in and out naturally, and just note your breathing rhythm.
- Now note the difference between your 'in' breath and your 'out' breath. Does one feel more comfortable than the other?

- Next, count how long an 'in' breath takes and how long an 'out' breath takes.
- If necessary, increase your 'out' breaths to make them longer. For instance, if you are counting slowly to the count of three for an 'in' breath, try aiming for a count of five for your 'out' breath (3/5). You can try extending this so that you breathe in for 7 and out for 11 (the 7/11 breathing exercise is well known), but if you find this too difficult go back to 3 and 5. The speed of counting doesn't matter, as long as the 'out' breath is longer than the 'in' breath.

It is important to ensure you are utilising deeper, diaphragm or belly breathing rather than higher, shallower breathing. You may find it helpful to breathe in through your nose and out through your mouth, paying particular attention to your stomach moving out when you inhale, and getting smaller when you exhale – put your hand on your stomach to feel this movement.

## Spiritual

Remember, shame is about how we perceive we exist in the minds of others. In the spiritual area, we are trying to connect with God and get a really true sense of His love. However, for those who are suffering with a high level of shame, this may seem very alien to them. To go back to the head/heart analogy – they may know in their head that God loves them, but in their heart they don't feel that at all and believe He views them very differently.

Interestingly, often the way that our parents related to us in childhood will be the way we perceive God as we grow up. Our relationship with our parents is what we transfer onto God, so if they were very angry, rejecting, or if we feel they abandoned us rather than soothing us, then we can project that onto God. We can begin to believe that He is angry, rejecting, abandoning. It is important to understand that when we become Christians we don't do so in a vacuum. As we have seen, we bring our past history and experience with us. Often the deepest healing comes from the spiritual area, and it can start when we understand our false views of who God is. As we said earlier, it can be a good idea for someone who is discovering this to take time to share and pray with someone they trust.

To aid our discussion of the spiritual area and how this can be affected by shame, Heather has found the theories of one more psychologist helpful: Frank Lake.[2] She has used a particular part of Lake's work with a lot of clients, as it draws on an understanding of the love of God.

Frank Lake (1914–1982) was a medical missionary in India, who then returned to England and trained in psychiatry. He is probably most famous for his book *Clinical Theology*, which was first published in 1966. In agreement with Bowlby's theories, Lake believed that mental health difficulties, including a person developing a deep sense of unworthiness, shame etc, can be traced back to childhood.[3] To help, he developed his theory of a dynamic cycle (see Appendix 2). Underpinning this theory are some key presuppositions, which are really helpful as they place a lot of the other theories we have been looking at into a Christian context.

First, Lake believed (as we do) that a lack of love in childhood can be overcome by the love of Christ. Second, he also argued that if you want to learn what a true model of health looks like, then you cannot look to any other person than Jesus Christ as your unique model of good mental health.

Lake used his observations on Jesus within Scripture as his model for human health.[4] Based on this, he created the dynamic cycle as a model of health. We have simplified the diagram; basically there are two input phases and two output phases.[5]

## THE TWO INPUT PHASES

### Acceptance

A mentally healthy person experiences love and acceptance with and from others. We see Jesus receiving from the Father perfect love and acceptance at His baptism: 'This is my Son, whom I love; with him I am well pleased' (Matt. 3:17). It is important to note that Jesus was affirmed by His Father *before* any ministry or achievement took place. A healthy sense of acceptance of ourselves is not based on what we do, but who we are (God's children).

### Sustenance

The second input phase is sustenance. Jesus knew His identity and it sustained Him. It gave Him a sense of wellbeing even in the most difficult of circumstances. For example, when He was led into the wilderness and tempted for 40 days (see Matt. 4:1–11), this came straight after His baptism, during which, as we have seen, God declared who He was. Knowing who He was helped Jesus to stay strong in the face of all the different tricks the devil tried to play on Him, which were based on questioning His identity ('If you are the Son of God...'; see vv3,6). We can see He was continually sustained by this knowledge, as He spoke of it to His disciples: 'I am in the Father and the Father is in me' (John 14:11).

Lake argued that successfully negotiating these two input phases leads to the development of a healthy personality, and in addition leads to the two output phases: status and achievement.

## THE TWO OUTPUT PHASES

### Status

According to Lake, if a person's input phase goes well, then they are able to be independent and mentally healthy and this leads to them having a sense of status. Jesus had a clear sense of status as the Son of God. When He was questioned directly by religious leaders as to whether He was the Messiah, Jesus' response was to say: 'I am' (Mark 14:62). The phrase 'I am' is the same that God used to reveal Himself to Moses: 'God said to Moses, "I AM WHO I AM. This is what you are to say to the Israelites: 'I am has sent me to you'"' (Exod. 3:14). By using the same term, Jesus was asserting that He is indeed the Son of God.

### Achievement

Having a sense of status leads to achievement. Submitting to the cross was Jesus' ultimate achievement, which involved laying down His life for us all. Knowing that that was His calling can give us comfort when we experience shame at the hands of others, as He was scorned, stripped and ultimately rejected by those He had come to save. He was at a place of being honest with His Father – in Gethsemane He asked: 'My Father, if it is possible, may this cup be taken from me' (Matt. 26:39) and yet, in the next sentence, was able to say: 'Yet not as I will, but as you will'. His sense of who He was, and knowing the love and total acceptance of His Father, enabled Him to achieve what He had been sent to earth to do.

Lake argued that a mentally healthy person is enabled to achieve – they are able to 'do' out of a place of knowing who they are – and are generously warm and reliable because they have experienced the Father's love.

Lake argued that this is the right way to go round the cycle – the healthy way. Problems occur when we go round the cycle the wrong way.

## THE WRONG WAY ROUND THE CYCLE

As the second cycle in the appendix shows, if you go around the cycle the wrong way:

**Acceptance** becomes a reward based on your activity and achievement.

**Achievement** becomes a performance – a person performs in order to feel they are acceptable.

**No status** – a person has no sense of status except for what they do and achieve.

**Sustenance** – close relationships are seen as a threat to security with the fear of rejection constantly present.

So, how does this relate to shame? Lake argued that people with deficits in their childhood relationships develop a deep sense of shame. In an attempt to win approval with God, they go round the circle constantly the wrong way to try and gain His acceptance. Indeed, Lake argued an overzealous attempt to win approval from God is not a virtue but more a neurotic symptom.[6]

Conversely, if you experience God's unconditional love, fully knowing and understanding that you are an adopted child of God, then you are brought into a cycle of wellbeing, which enables you to go round the dynamic cycle the right way. Fully understanding our identity in Christ is such a vital part of enabling a healthy approach to our relationships to God and others (see below). It is important to reiterate that He loves us fully and totally, exactly as we are in this moment. We do not need to strive for His approval or love.

## Activity

Can you identify times when you have gone round the cycle the wrong way? What do you think caused that? What can you put in place to change this going forward?

If you know you have a tendency to try and earn God's favour, sharing that with someone you trust can be helpful, so that they can be praying for and encouraging you to go back the right way round the cycle. And if you have been approached by someone who recognises this in themselves, or you have been able to point this out to them, do make sure you continue to support and pray for them.

Martin was a young man Heather had as a client just after he had completed training for Christian ministry. When she showed him the dynamic cycle, it profoundly impacted him as it was the first time he understood that he was trying to earn God's love. He recognised that he was going round the cycle the wrong way. For years afterwards he would send Heather a postcard of where he had been on holiday. He would try to find a picture of a lake wherever he was, and would put the same message each time: 'Still swimming around the lake the right way.'

The dynamic cycle also profoundly impacted Heather personally, just before she started counselling training. She and her husband had just changed churches and, not long after, her husband was asked to become a part of the leadership team. They were invited to a leadership conference. Heather remembers arriving, feeling very much that she was trying to be the leader's wife, dressed smartly with her Bible at the ready, and then the speaker started to talk about the dynamic cycle and she immediately broke down into tears as healing came. Heather had a difficult childhood, where she gained the message from her parents that she had to achieve in order to be good enough and to be loved. Heather became a Christian at 16, having come from a non-Christian household. She took her baggage of trying to achieve in order to be loved into her faith journey. But as the speaker shared, she suddenly realised in a moment that she didn't have to earn God's love, and that He loved her for who she was. For those struggling with shame, understanding that God loves us for who we are is a profoundly healing way to recover from the depths of shame.

## Knowing who we are in Christ

Lake talked about the importance of basing our sense of a healthy human on Jesus, and it follows that really cementing our knowledge of who we are both *because of* and *in* Him will aid us as we seek to step away from shame towards fuller healing. We have said that it is necessary for the truth to permeate not just our heads but our hearts too, but also recognise the importance of feeding ourselves on that truth through gazing on the love of God and spending time with Him regularly. It is in His presence that we are most reminded of His love, and our inheritance as His sons and daughters.

When we are struggling with deep shame, it can be hard for us to do this and receive God's love. We want to do what Adam and Eve did in the beginning: hide from God. But Jesus came to set us free from all that holds us, including our shame. He died so that we might become free – free to be all He intended us to be. What is amazing is that God knows how much we can struggle with this; the Bible is full of verses right from the start to the end that reveal what He thinks about us and who He says we are. As we meditate on those, spend time resting in His presence and use the truth of what He says about us to combat any unhelpful thoughts we have (as we saw in Chapter 6), we can learn to accept who God says we are. As we mentioned previously, we don't do this in our own strength, but with the help of the Holy Spirit, who has been put 'in our hearts as a deposit, guaranteeing what is to come' (2 Cor. 1:22).

The more we gaze on the love of God and focus on who we are in Christ, the more we will find shame starts to diminish. Yes, it is an ongoing challenge, but here are some great verses that remind you of who you are in Christ. Meditating on them, even reading them aloud daily, is a great habit to form as it gives you tools you can use to combat unhelpful thoughts:

'Since then you have been raised with Christ... you died, and your life is now hidden with Christ in God' (Col. 3:1,3). We are not defined by successes or failures, but by the fact that God identifies us as His own, which He did by setting His 'seal of ownership on us' (2 Cor. 1:22). He loves us so much that He rejoices over us with singing (Zeph. 3:17).

We have now become known as children of God: 'to those who believed in his name, he gave the right to become children of God' (John 1:12). Incredibly, we are not only Jesus' siblings now, but His friends too, and He willingly shares the Father's heart with us: 'I no longer call you servants, because a servant does not know his master's business. Instead, I have called you friends, for everything that I learned from my Father I have made known to you' (John 15:15). These are such incredible truths, aren't they?

## The importance of prayer

Throughout this book we have talked about understanding the reasons why we can struggle with shame, and provided various practical suggestions for working through shame. Within every aspect of this process, we can include God – and through prayer He can provide us with fresh insights that are specifically for our own situations (or those we are helping). As we have said before, asking a friend to stand with us in prayer can provide wonderful support too. It can also be helpful to learn to talk to God whenever we sense we are beginning to respond unhealthily to the threat of shame. You may want to take time to draft something now that you can utilise in those moments.

Reflection

In every aspect of our lives, whether struggling with shame, facing other difficulties or being in a season of peace and calm, there is nothing more important than dwelling on God's love for us as individuals. It is the fuel that enables us to be all that He created us to be.

Read through the love letter from God (Appendix 3), and then respond in any way that feels appropriate. (You could perhaps turn to worship and prayer, or write a love letter back – maybe writing out some of the verses shared above in a journal would be helpful.)

## Activity

Take some time to think back over what you have learned during the course of the book. What is your biggest takeaway for yourself? For those you are helping? Make a note of these and come back to check in a week's time to see if you have applied them well. (You may want to then check back again in a few months.)

As we end this book, we wanted to share with you the apostle Paul's prayer, as it is our prayer for you too. Think about what it could mean for you to fully grasp God's love as you read:

> 'I pray that out of his glorious riches he may strengthen you with power through his Spirit in your inner being, so that Christ may dwell in your hearts through faith. And I pray that you, being rooted and established in love, may have power, together with all the Lord's holy people, to grasp how wide and long and high and deep is the love of Christ, and to know this love that surpasses knowledge – that you may be filled to the measure of all the fullness of God.'
>
> Ephesians 3:16–19

Our ultimate healing from shame lies in the truth of this prayer: that we are deeply and dearly loved by God. Whatever our past, whatever our shame, we are His and nothing can ever separate us from His love.

## Prayer

*Lord, thank You for everything that I have been learning through this book. Understanding more about myself and others – our triggers for shame and why we believe the things we do – is definitely the first step in being able to overcome in this area. I pray that You will guide and direct me in the coming days and years into more freedom from shame, and help me show others how to step into this too, so that we can embrace our full identity in You. Amen.*

# Appendices

## Appendix 1:
## The Waverley Integrative Framework

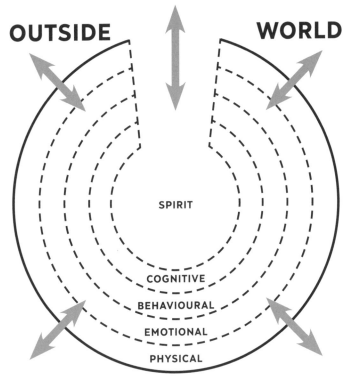

## Appendix 2: The Dynamic Cycle

**2. SUSTENANCE**
we are God's
children, dearly loved

**1. ACCEPTANCE**
we are accepted
and loved for
who we are

**3. STATUS**
we can be all that
God has called us to
be, sure in His love

**4. ACHIEVEMENT**
we can achieve God's
plan for our lives

In shame, we follow the cycle – but the wrong way round.

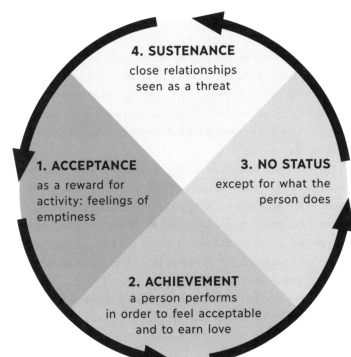

## Appendix 3: Father's Love Letter

*An intimate message from God to you.*

My Child,

You may not know me, but I know everything about you (Psa. 139:1).

I know when you sit down and when you rise up (Psa. 139:2). I am familiar with all your ways (Psa. 139:3). Even the very hairs on your head are numbered (Matt. 10:29–31). For you were made in my image (Gen. 1:27). In me you live and move and have your being, for you are my offspring (Acts 17:28).

I knew you even before you were conceived (Jer. 1:4–5). I chose you when I planned creation (Eph. 1:11–12). You were not a mistake, for all your days are written in my book (Psa. 139:15–16). I determined the exact time of your birth and where you would live (Acts 17:26). You are fearfully and wonderfully made (Psa. 139:14). I knit you together in your mother's womb (Psa. 139:13). And brought you forth on the day you were born (Psa. 71:6).

I have been misrepresented by those who don't know me (John 8:41–44). I am not distant and angry, but am the complete expression of love (1 John 4:16). And it is my desire to lavish my love on you. Simply because you are my child and I am your Father (1 John 3:1).

I offer you more than your earthly father ever could (Matt. 7:11). For I am the perfect Father (Matt. 5:48).

Every good gift that you receive comes from my hand (James 1:17). For I am your provider and I meet all your needs (Matt. 6:31–33). My plan for your future has always been filled with hope (Jer. 29:11). Because I love you with an everlasting love (Jer. 31:3).

My thoughts toward you are countless as the sand on the seashore (Psa. 139:17–18). And I rejoice over you with singing (Zeph. 3:17).

I will never stop doing good to you (Jer. 32:40). For you are my treasured possession (Exod. 19:5).

I desire to establish you with all my heart and all my soul (Jer. 32:41). And I want to show you great and marvelous things (Jer. 33:3).

If you seek me with all your heart, you will find me (Deut. 4:29).

Delight in me and I will give you the desires of your heart (Psa. 37:4). For it is I who gave you those desires (Phil. 2:13).

I am able to do more for you than you could possibly imagine (Eph. 3:20). For I am your greatest encourager (2 Thess. 2:16–17).

I am also the Father who comforts you in all your troubles (2 Cor. 1:3–4). When you are brokenhearted, I am close to you (Psa. 34:18). As a shepherd carries a lamb, I have carried you close to my heart (Isa. 40:11).

One day I will wipe away every tear from your eyes. And I'll take away all the pain you have suffered on this earth (Rev. 21:3–4).

I am your Father, and I love you even as I love my Son, Jesus (John 17:23). For in Jesus, my love for you is revealed (John 17:26). He is the exact representation of my being (Heb. 1:3). He came to demonstrate that I am for you, not against you (Rom. 8:31). And to tell you that I am not counting your sins. Jesus died so that you and I could be reconciled (2 Cor. 5:18–19).

His death was the ultimate expression of my love for you (1 John 4:10). I gave up everything I loved that I might gain your love (Rom. 8:31–32).

If you receive the gift of my Son Jesus, you receive me (1 John 2:23). And nothing will ever separate you from my love again (Rom. 8:38–39).

Come home and I'll throw the biggest party heaven has ever seen (Luke 15:7).

I have always been Father, and will always be Father (Eph. 3:14–15). My question is... Will you be my child (John 1:12–13)?

I am waiting for you (Luke 15:11–32).

Love, Your Dad... Almighty God

© 1999 Father Heart Communications

# Endnotes

**CHAPTER 1**

[1]Paul Gilbert and Sue Procter, 'Compassionate mind training for people with high shame and self-criticism: overview and pilot study of a group therapy approach', *Clinical Psychology & Psychotherapy*, Vol 13, Issue 6, 2006, pp353–379

[2]S.B. Lupis, 'Role of Shame and Body Esteem in Cortisol Stress responses', *Journal of Behavioral Medicine*, Vol 39, Issue 2, 2016, pp262–275

[3]Mayo Clinic Staff, 'Chronic stress puts your health at risk', 2016, found at mayoclinic.org (Accessed January 2019)

[4]R. Thomas and S. Parker, 'Toward A Theological Understanding of Shame', *Journal of Psychology and Christianity*, Vol 23, Issue 2, 2004, pp176–182

[5]etymonline.com/word/shame (Accessed March 2019)

[6]D. Kollareth, J.M. Fernandez-Dols and J.A. Russell, 'Shame as a Culture Specific Emotion Concept', *Journal of Cognition and Culture*, Vol 18, Issue 3–4, 2018, pp274–292

[7]R. Thomas and S. Parker, 'Toward A Theological Understanding of Shame', *Journal of Psychology and Christianity*, Vol 23, Issue 2, 2004, pp176–182

[8]*Ibid*

[9]Heather Churchill and Wendy Bray, *Insight into Helping Survivors of Childhood Sexual Abuse* (Farnham: CWR, 2012)

[10]en.oxforddictionaries.com/definition/guilt (Accessed March 2019)

[11]en.oxforddictionaries.com/definition/shame (Accessed March 2019)

[12]For example, see P. Woolley, 'Shame' in J.D. Douglas, N. Hillyer, and D. Wood (eds), *New Bible Dictionary* (Leicester: Intervarsity Press, 1996). See also S. Pattison, *Shame: Theory, Therapy, Theology* (Cambridge: Cambridge University Press, 2000)

[13]R.Thomas and S. Parker, 'Toward A Theological Understanding of Shame', *Journal of Psychology and Christianity*, Vol 23, Issue 2, 2004, p176

[14]Paul Gilbert, 'Shame in Psychotherapy and the Role of Compassion Focused Therapy' in R. Dearing and J.P. Tangney (eds.), *Shame in the Therapy Hour* (Washington DC, USA: American Psychological Association, 2011)

[15]Brené Brown, *Shame v. Guilt*, 14 January 2013, brenebrown.com/blog/2013/01/14/shame-v-guilt (Accessed November 2017)

[16]*Ibid*

[17]*Ibid*

[18]Paul Gilbert, and S. Procter, 'Compassionate mind training for people with high shame and self-criticism: overview and pilot study of a group therapy approach', *Clinical Psychology & Psychotherapy*, Vol 13, Issue 6, 2006, pp353–379

[19]Brené Brown, *Shame v. Guilt*, 14 January 2013, brenebrown.com/blog/2013/01/14/shame-v-guilt (Accessed November 2017)

[20]Judith Lewis Herman, 'Shattered Shame States and their repair', found at challiance.org (Accessed November 2017)

**CHAPTER 2**

[1]R. Mills, 'Taking stock of the developmental literature on shame', *Developmental Review*, Vol 25, Issue 1, 2005, pp26–63

[2]R. Mills, P. Hastings, L. Serbin, D. Stack, J. Abela, K. Arbeau, and D. Lall, 'Depressogenic Thinking and Shame Proneness in the Development of Internalizing Problems', *Child Psychiatry and Human Development*, Vol 46, Issue 2, 2015, pp194–208

[3] J. Bradshaw, *Healing the shame that binds you* (Florida: Health Communications, 2005) p8

[4] P. Hultberg, 'Shame – A Hidden Emotion', *Journal of Analytical Psychology*, Vol 33, 1988, pp109–126

[5] R. Metcalf, 'The Truth of Shame Consciousness in Freud and Phenomenology', *Journal of Phenomenological Psychology*, Vol 31, Issue 1, 2000, pp1–18

[6] *Ibid*

[7] C.S. Carver and M.F. Scheier, *Perspectives on Personality*, Fourth Edition (London: Allyn Books, 2000)

[8] *Ibid*

[9] Judith Lewis Herman, 'Shattered Shame States and their repair', found at challiance.org (Accessed November 2017)

[10] John Bowlby, *Attachment and Loss: Separation, Anxiety and Anger: Volume 2* (London: Pimlico, 1998)

[11] *Ibid*

[12] *Ibid*

[13] R. Mills, 'Taking stock of the developmental literature on shame', *Developmental Review*, Vol 25, Issue 1, 2005, pp26–63

[14] Paul Gilbert, 'Shame in Psychotherapy and the Role of Compassion Focused Therapy' in R. Dearing and J.P. Tangney (eds.), *Shame in the Therapy Hour* (Washington DC, USA: American Psychological Association, 2011)

[15] K. Goss and S. Allan, 'The development and application of compassion-focused therapy for eating disorders', *British Journal of Clinical Psychology*, Vol 53, Issue 1, 2014, pp62–77

[16] Paul Gilbert, 'Shame in Psychotherapy and the Role of Compassion Focused Therapy' in R. Dearing and J.P. Tangney (eds.) *Shame in the Therapy Hour* (Washington DC, USA: American Psychological Association, 2011)

## CHAPTER 3

[1] Paul Gilbert, 'Introducing Compassion Focused Therapy', 2010, found at compassionatemind.co.uk (Accessed January 2019)

[2] *Ibid*

[3] *Ibid*

[4] D. Greenberger and C.A. Padesky, *Mind over Mood: Change the way you feel by changing the way you think* (New York, USA: Guilford Press, 1995)

[5] Paul Gilbert, 'Shame in Psychotherapy and the Role of Compassion Focused Therapy' in R. Dearing and J.P. Tangney (eds.), *Shame in the Therapy Hour* (Washington DC, USA: American Psychological Association, 2011)

[6] R. Stott, 'When head and heart do not agree: A theoretical and clinical analysis of Rational-Emotional Dissociation (RED) in Cognitive Therapy', *Journal of Cognitive Psychotherapy*, Vol 21, Issue 1, 2007, pp37–50

[7] Paul Gilbert, 'Shame in Psychotherapy and the Role of Compassion Focused Therapy' in R. Dearing and J.P. Tangney (eds.), *Shame in the Therapy Hour* (Washington DC, USA: American Psychological Association, 2011)

[8] Paul Gilbert, 'Introducing Compassion Focused Therapy', 2010, found at compassionatemind.co.uk (Accessed January 2019)

[9] *Ibid*

[10] Paul Gilbert, 'The origins and nature of compassion focused therapy', *British Journal of Clinical Psychology*, Vol 53, Issue 1, 2014, pp6–41

[11] *Ibid*

[12] *Ibid*

[13]Paul Gilbert, 'Introducing Compassion Focused Therapy', 2010, found at compassionatemind.co.uk (Accessed January 2019)

[14] *Ibid*

[15]N. Eisenberger, M.D. Lieberman and K.D. Williams, 'Does Rejection Hurt? An FMRI Study of Social Exclusion', *Science*, Vol 302, Issue 5643, 2003, pp290–292

## CHAPTER 4

[1]Paul Gilbert, 'Introducing Compassion Focused Therapy', 2010, found at compassionatemind.co.uk (Accessed January 2019)

[2] *Ibid*

[3]Goss, K. & Allan, S., 'The development and application of compassion-focused therapy for eating disorders', *British Journal of Clinical Psychology*, Vol 53, Issue 1, 2014, pp62–77

[4]Paul Gilbert, 'Introducing Compassion Focused Therapy', 2010, found at compassionatemind.co.uk (Accessed January 2019)

[5]Paul Gilbert, 'Shame in Psychotherapy and the Role of Compassion Focused Therapy' in R. Dearing and J.P. Tangney (eds.), *Shame in the Therapy Hour* (Washington DC, USA: American Psychological Association, 2011), p340

[6] *Ibid*

[7]Paul Gilbert, 'The origins and nature of compassion focused therapy', *British Journal of Clinical Psychology*, Vol 53, Issue 1, 2014, pp6–41

[8]J. A. Schibsted, 'A recovery strategy for workaholic pastors', *Dissertation Abstracts International Section A*, 55 (8-A), 1995

[9]Paul Gilbert, 'The origins and nature of compassion focused therapy', *British Journal of Clinical Psychology*, Vol 53, Issue 1, 2014, pp6–41

[10]Markus MacGill, 'What is the link between love and oxytocin?', 2017, found at medicalnewstoday.com (Accessed December 2018)

[11]L. Cozolino, *Why Therapy Works: Using our Minds to Change our Brains* (New York, USA: W.W. Norton and Company, 2016)

[12]Paul Gilbert, 'Introducing Compassion Focused Therapy', 2010, found at compassionatemind.co.uk (Accessed January 2019)

## CHAPTER 5

[1]If you are interested in exploring this further, the work of Richard Schwartz on the manager, firefighter and exile parts is relevant. See Richard Schwartz, *Internal Family Systems Theory* (London: Guilford Press, 1995). See also Janina Fisher, *Healing the Fragmented Selves of Trauma Survivors: Overcoming Internal Self-Alienation* (London: Routledge, 2017)

[2]Janina Fisher, *Healing the Fragmented Selves of Trauma Survivors: Overcoming Internal Self-Alienation* (London: Routledge, 2017) p19

[3] *Ibid*, p69

[4] *Ibid*, p69

[5] *Ibid*

[6]Janina Fisher, 'The treatment of structural dissociation in chronically traumatized patients', available at janinafisher.com (Accessed January 2018)

[7]Janina Fisher, *Healing the Fragmented Selves of Trauma Survivors: Overcoming Internal Self-Alienation* (London: Routledge, 2017) pp65–75

[8]Ibid, p80

[9]Jon Kabat Zinn, *Wherever you go there you are: Mindfulness meditation in everyday life* (New York, USA: Hyperion, 1994)

[10]J. Collicutt, R. Bretherton and J. Brickman, *Being Mindful, Being Christian: A Guide to Mindful Discipleship* (Oxford: Grand Rapids, 2016). See also S. Tan, 'Mindfulness and acceptance-based cognitive behavioral therapies: Empirical evidence and clinical applications from a Christian perspective', *Journal of Psychology and Christianity*, Vol 30, Issue 3, 2011, pp243–249

[11]Paul Gilbert and Dennis Tirch, 'Emotional Memory, Mindfulness and Compassion', in *Clinical Handbook of Mindfulness* (New York, USA: Springer Science, 2009) pp99–110

[12]Janina Fisher, *Healing the Fragmented Selves of Trauma Survivors: Overcoming Internal Self-Alienation* (London: Routledge, 2017) p80

[13]J. Arch and M. Craske, 'Mechanisms of mindfulness: Emotion regulation following a focused breathing induction', *Behaviour Research and Therapy*, Vol 44, Issue 12, 2006, pp1849–1858

## CHAPTER 6

[1]Paul Gilbert and Sue Procter, 'Compassionate mind training for people with high shame and self-criticism: overview and pilot study of a group therapy approach', *Clinical Psychology & Psychotherapy*, Vol 13, Issue 6, 2006, pp353–379

[2]Taken and adapted from Deborah Lee, *The Compassionate Mind Approach to Recovering from Trauma using Compassion Focused Therapy* (London: Robinson, 2012), pp137–138

[3]Shelley Taylor, 'Tend and Befriend: Biobehavioral Bases of Affiliation Under Stress', *Current Directions in Psychological Science*, Vol 15, Issue 6, 2006, pp273–277

[4]Deborah Lee, *The Compassionate Mind Approach to Recovering from Trauma using Compassion Focused Therapy* (London: Robinson, 2012)

[5]John Bradshaw, *Healing the shame that binds you* (Florida: Health Communications, 2005)

[6]Chris Ledger and Claire Musters, *Insight into Self-Acceptance* (Farnham: CWR, 2016)

[7]Paul Gilbert, 'Compassionate letter writing', found at compassionatemind.co.uk (Accessed December 2017)

[8]Deborah Lee, *The Compassionate Mind Approach to Recovering from Trauma using Compassion Focused Therapy* (London: Robinson, 2012) p180

[9]Paul Gilbert, 'Building a Compassionate Image' found at compassionatemind.co.uk (Accessed December 2017)

## CHAPTER 7

[1]This explanation, and the accompanying breathing exercise, has been taken and slightly adapted from Chris Ledger and Claire Musters, *Insight into Burnout* (Farnham: CWR, 2016) pp75,88–89

[2]Frank Lake, *Clinical Theology, A Theological and Psychiatric Basis to Clinical Pastoral Care* (London: Emeth Press, 2006)

[3]Ibid

[4]Ibid

[5]For more on this, see bridgepastoral.org.uk/dynamic-cycle.htm (Accessed January 2017)

[6]Frank Lake, *Clinical Theology, A Theological and Psychiatric Basis to Clinical Pastoral Care* (London: Emeth Press, 2006)

# Insight series

## Handling issues that are often feared, ignored or misunderstood.

### Courses

CWR's Insight courses draw on real-life case studies, biblical examples and counselling practices to offer insight on important topics, including depression, anxiety, stress, anger and self-acceptance. These courses has been developed by CWR's experienced tutors in response to the great need to help people understand and work through key issues.

These invaluable teaching days are designed both for those who would like to come for their own benefit and for those who seek to support or understand people facing particular issues.

To find out more and to book, visit **cwr.org.uk/courses** or call 01252 784719

## Books

CWR's Insight books give biblical and professional insight into some of the key issues that many people face today but are often feared, ignored or misunderstood. Covering a range of topics including anxiety, stress, bereavement and eating disorders, these books are suitable for both those facing the issues involved, as well as those supporting others. Each book includes case studies and practical insights.

**Insight into Addiction**
ISBN: 978-1-85345-661-9

**Insight into Anger**
ISBN: 978-1-78259-730-8

**Insight into Anxiety**
ISBN: 978-1-85345-662-6

**Insight into Depression**
ISBN: 978-1-85345-538-4

**Insight into Eating Disorders**
ISBN: 978-1-85345-791-3

**Insight into Self-Esteem**
ISBN: 978-1-85345-663-3

**Insight into Self-Harm**
ISBN: 978-1-85345-960-3

 ALSO AVAILABLE AS EBOOK/KINDLE

For a complete list of all titles available in this series,
visit **cwr.org.uk/insight**
Available online or from Christian bookshops.

# LET'S TALK...

## WHEN WAS THE LAST TIME YOU HAD AN HONEST CONVERSATION?

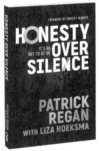
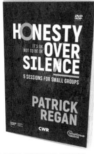

ISBN: 978-1-78259-833-6  EAN: 5027957-001732

Patrick Regan OBE is the CEO of Kintsugi Hope, and the founder of the urban youth work charity XLP.

Honesty Over Silence seeks to break the stigma around mental health and encourage open conversations that bring both understanding and hope. Powerful true stories from Patrick Regan and others about some of life's hardest challenges show how the strength in sharing honestly helps us to grow into the people God created us to be.

Based on the book, the five-session DVD includes interviews and discussion starters, making it ideal for use in small groups.

*'It's going to provoke ten thousand honest conversations, helping to bring healing, hope and understanding to many who currently suffer in silence'* – **Pete Greig**, founder of 24-7 Prayer

**cwr.org.uk/HOS**
Available online or from Christian bookshops.

Courses and seminars

Waverley Abbey College

Publishing and media

Conference facilities

# Transforming lives

CWR's vision is to enable people to experience personal transformation through applying God's Word to their lives and relationships.

Our Bible-based training and resources help people around the world to:

- Grow in their walk with God
- Understand and apply Scripture to their lives
- Resource themselves and their church
- Develop pastoral care and counselling skills
- Train for leadership
- Strengthen relationships, marriage and family life and much more.

Our insightful writers provide daily Bible reading notes and other resources for all ages, and our experienced course designers and presenters have gained an international reputation for excellence and effectiveness.

CWR's Training and Conference Centre in Surrey, England, provides excellent facilities in idyllic settings – ideal for both learning and spiritual refreshment.

**CWR** **Applying God's Word**
to everyday life and relationships

WR, Waverley Abbey House,
averley Lane, Farnham,
urrey GU9 8EP, UK

**elephone:** +44 (0)1252 784700
**mail:** info@cwr.org.uk
**ebsite:** cwr.org.uk

egistered Charity No. 294387
ompany Registration No. 1990308